The Citizen Solution

The Citizen Solution
How You Can Make a Difference

HARRY C. BOYTE

Foreword by Don Shelby

MINNESOTA HISTORICAL SOCIETY PRESS

in cooperation with the KETTERING FOUNDATION PRESS

www.mhspress.org

The Minnesota Historical Society Press is a member of the Association of American University Presses.

Manufactured in Canada

10 9 8 7 6 5 4 3 2 1

♾ The paper used in this publication meets the minimum requirements of the American National Standard for Information Sciences — Permanence for Printed Library Materials, ANSI Z39.48 — 1984.

International Standard Book Number
ISBN 13: 978-0-87351-610-5 (paper)
ISBN 10: 0-87351-610-9 (paper)

Library of Congress Cataloging-in-Publication Data
Boyte, Harry Chatten, 1945 –
The citizen solution : how you can make a difference /
Harry C. Boyte ; foreword by Don Shelby.
    p.   cm.
Includes bibliographical references and index.
ISBN-13: 978-0-87351-610-5 (pbk. : alk. paper)
ISBN-10: 0-87351-610-9 (pbk. : alk. paper)
    1. Political participation — United States. 2. Citizens' associations — United States. I. Title.
JK1764.B694 2008
323.' 0240973 — dc22
2007049707

The publication of this book was supported through a generous grant from the Richardson B. Okie Fund for Public Affairs.

Acknowledgments

The Citizen Solution grows out of a long collaboration between the Center for Democracy and Citizenship (CDC) and our colleagues at the Kettering Foundation. Kettering has supported many CDC research projects into topics as diverse as populism, community-based learning, patterns of decision making in immigrant communities, young people's civic education, how people shift from seeing themselves as consumers to seeing themselves as powerful public actors and problem solvers, low-income parent involvement in children's education, the civic mission of higher education, and public scholarship. Beyond specific research efforts, Kettering and its wide-ranging, international network of associates and partners has created a remarkable learning community for exchange and development of ideas about democracy, citizenship, politics, and public work. I am deeply appreciative. I want to thank especially David Mathews, president of Kettering, for outstanding intellectual leadership on questions of deliberation, public work, and education; John Dedrick, director of programs at Kettering, who is a fine political theorist with keen insights into the temper of our times and a superb critic of my writing; and Debi Witte and David Brown, who coordinated the several-year conversation on the relationship between higher education and democracy described in *Agent of Democracy: Higher Education and the HEX Journey.*

As *The Citizen Solution* has been drafted and redrafted, I have benefited from the thoughts of many other partners and colleagues, too numerous to mention. But I want to thank Nan Skelton, Bill Doherty, Dennis Donovan, Elaine Eschenbacher, Jim Lewis, Ellen Tveit, Gary Cunningham, Al Quie, Atum Azzahir, Tim Kamenar, Doran Schrantz, Jeanne Ayers, Catherine Eichers, Peter Levine, Xolela Mangcu, and Michael Edwards for their regular and continuing conversations about this project and its themes. Carmen Sirianni and Fiona Donald went through the entire manuscript and made many helpful suggestions. And I am very grateful to Marilyn Ziebarth at the Minnesota Historical Society Press, for her assiduous editing.

I owe the most, far and away, to Marie-Louise Ström, my life partner and amazing coworker. Marie suffered late night discussions and early morning wake ups. She read many drafts. And she brought her demanding expectations and passion for democracy education and development to bear throughout. *The Citizen Solution* would not have seen the light of day without her.

Contents

Foreword

DON SHELBY

The Citizen Solution: How You Can Make a Difference is a deceptively simple title for a book. Most of us cut our civics baby teeth on the notion that we, the people, navigate our ship of state. What, then, could this book teach us? Harry Boyte doesn't teach us, so much as remind us, that citizens produce our society and government and do not simply consume its culture and services.

The Citizen Solution conveys its message by examples, and as a storyteller I learned long ago that people learn lessons best when lessons are wrapped in stories or parables. Having spent a good portion of my professional career in journalism bemoaning the loss of public participation in our own lives, I am thrilled to see Boyte provide case after case of citizen problem solving right here under our noses.

Most of us believe we know what citizenship means, but Boyte shows us, in this wonderfully readable book, what citizenship looks like in action. We need the examples, because we don't fully comprehend the real meaning of this common, and perhaps, overused term: citizenship. My own notion, now informed fully by this book, comes from my third-grade teacher, Marjorie Quick. While it may come as a surprise to younger readers, school report cards once made room for grades in citizenship. When I handed over my report card to my father, I knew what he would do. He would look past the grades in English, Math, and History and flip the card over to see how I scored in Citizenship. The only acceptable grade was an A.

Once, in the third grade, I got a B in Citizenship. My father was ashamed. I was confused, because the truth was that I had no idea what citizenship was nor how I was being judged. The next day I asked Mrs. Quick, "What is citizenship, anyway?" She smiled beatifically, as though she'd been waiting a very long time for the question. "Honey," she said (in those days, teachers could use endearments for their young charges), "Citizenship means how well you work with others. First you try to become the best person you can be. Then you help others to do the same. Then, together, you work to make this the best classroom in the school. If everyone is a good citizen, working together, think what a nice school we will have. Then, when you are older, you will work with others to make a good neighborhood, community, and town. Then, what I hope is that you will grow into an adult who will work with others to make a better state, and a better country, and even a better world."

I've never heard a better description of citizenship, nor have I ever needed one. Mrs. Quick's kind of clarity has, over these past fifty years, been lost to many of us. Citizenship has been conflated with nationality, politics, and reductionist patriotism. In *The Citizen Solution: How You Can Make a Difference,* Harry Boyte makes plain what working well with others looks like and what a nice place we can make if we follow, and replicate, the citizenship of the men and women and groups highlighted here. And, like Mrs. Quick, he gives us a little homework to drive home the lessons.

When I finished this book I was reminded of the words of another woman, a citizen warrior for women's rights, Hannah Whitall Smith, who said, "There are people who make things happen, and there are those who watch things happen. And there are those who wonder what happened." Harry Boyte obviously likes people who make things happen.

Marjorie Quick is long gone, but her simple lessons live on in my heart, and in some small way, I hope, in my neighborhood. Harry Boyte would have loved Mrs. Quick. Mrs. Quick would have loved this book.

The Citizen Solution

Introduction
Beyond Slash-and-Burn Politics

The Citizen Solution tells about an emerging citizen movement that is beginning to overcome people's feelings of powerlessness and hopelessness about the large problems facing us. *The Citizen Solution* describes what makes for effective civic action and civic organizations through which successful action can be sustained. It also shows why you are vital to this movement and what you can glean from its stories — successes and failures alike — for your civic work. Each chapter concludes with a civic-skills section and tips on how to develop them. *The Citizen Solution* is a resource for citizens to use in solving problems, building people's organizations, and making a better world. It draws on twenty years of work by civic organizers at the Humphrey Institute of Public Affairs and partners in Minnesota and beyond, as well as the efforts of many others.

Stirrings of effective civic action are strong in Minnesota because of its rich history of citizens' taking self-reliant, cooperative action and working together on public problems — not looking to government or experts to fix things. In Minnesota a new generation of creative innovators has renewed this tradition, creating powerful people's organizations through which civic work can be sustained over time. There is also a citizen movement developing across the nation and the world.

This civic movement is largely invisible to most people. Much better known are the problems that give rise to today's civic efforts. For a number of years, scholars, social commentators, religious leaders, and regular citizens have worried about the loss of community ties. Many decry the coarsening of public life, the dominance of get-rich-quick and look-out-for-number-one values, and the loss of a sense of the common good.

Jonathan Sacks, chief rabbi of the United Hebrew Congregations of Great Britain, gave wise expression to such concerns in *The Politics of Hope*. Sacks contrasted the socially chaotic and hopeless circumstances of today's poor minorities in England with his own family's Jewish background in eastern Europe. His family was economically impoverished but rich in cultural and relational resources. In contrast, young people in many low-income communities he has visited live in a world of few stable civic networks and eroding community values. In response, Sacks called for a broad effort to renew civic values and community life. "Every age has its characteristic preoccupations," he writes. Since the Enlightenment, a central concern of intellectuals has been to create space for individuals "to be themselves" against the weight of constricting tradition, stuffy Victorian codes, or, in the twentieth century, totalitarian communist and fascist belief systems. Yet times have changed. "As the twentieth century draws to a close . . . it would be fairer to say that we stand in the opposite situation. In today's liberal democracies, it is not that we are too much together but that we are too much alone and seek to learn again how to connect with others in lasting and rewarding ways."[1]

Concern about the erosion of community in the modern world has been voiced across partisan divides for more than a decade. Both Bill Clinton and George W. Bush, for all their differences, declared themselves to be "communitarians," a school of political thought concerned with renewing community. Clinton ran for president in 1992 on a platform of "responsibility, community, and opportunity." He gave his

1995 State of the Union address on the New Covenant, calling for a re-birth of the work of citizenship. Similarly, Bush made citizen-service the centerpiece of his 2001 inaugural address, using phrases that Clinton had used in his 1995 State of the Union speech. "I ask you to seek a common good beyond your comfort," Bush proclaimed, "to be citizens, not spectators, to serve your nation, beginning with your neighborhood."[2]

Both presidents came up against—and in some ways also contributed to—a politics headed in the opposite direction, which has reshaped the national public debate. It shows the large obstacles that the citizen movement faces.

Slash-and-Burn Politics

In the early 1990s, the Humphrey Institute's Center for Democracy and Citizenship organized Washington meetings on "improving politics." We found wide responsiveness because our discussions drew on several years of concern about the erosion of community and civic life in America. There was also a growing interest in new approaches to effective public problem solving. E. J. Dionne's 1991 book, *Why Americans Hate Politics*, struck a chord with many political and civic leaders with his argument that collaborative governance and effective action to address the nation's problems were undermined by divisive partisanship.

In this environment, we were able to bring civic organizers, political leaders, and key journalists together in Washington. We later developed a bipartisan project called the New Citizenship with the White House Domestic Policy Council, looking at examples of government agencies that were working successfully with communities on issues like housing, crime control, and restoring the environment. President Clinton based his New Covenant State of the Union address in 1995 partly on this project, after a Camp David meeting in which we reported on our findings.

When Clinton encountered resistance among the Washington establishment to the New Covenant message, he quickly backtracked and adopted a strategy that ultimately made enemies of both congressional Democrats and Republicans, the opposite of his calls for "the work of citizenship." This experience taught us that civic messages need to have strong civic support on the ground if they are to be sustained in the face of opposition.

Today there is much more civic organizing and action. But the over-all political trend has become what might be termed slash-and-burn politics, after the agricultural techniques that produce quick harvests but ravage the environment. Karl Rove, architect of George W. Bush's political career, was a master of this technique. As David Frum, for a time President Bush's chief speechwriter, described it in the *New York Times,* Rove helped to crystallize a "politics that aimed at winning elections [and] treated the problems of governance as secondary."[3] Reporter Adam Nagourney elaborated, "Mr. Rove has to a considerable extent changed the way politics are played. Modeled on his example, campaigns have become more disciplined in driving simple, often negative messages. They . . . identify the vulnerabilities of potential opponents, and they do extensive negative research as they prepare to exploit those. . . . And they methodically use marketing and other data to identify potential supporters and get them to the polls."[4]

Rove may have brought slash-and-burn techniques to a new level of sophistication, but he did not invent them. Their origins are to be found in issue campaigns around "good causes" like the environment, based on techniques of mass mobilization like door-to-door canvassing and direct mail appeals. Today, slash-and-burn politics is found across the spectrum, including the issue campaigns of groups on the left. All rely on a formula that involves finding an enemy to demonize, whipping up emotions with inflammatory language, shutting down critical thought in the process, and projecting the fiction that we have to look to leaders to solve things for us. Because slash-and-burn techniques often "work" in the narrow terms in which issues or elections are fought out, candidates and campaigns on both sides experience pressures to adopt them.

Slash-and-burn politics works not only because of new techniques but also because of divisions among the people. While there are many new forms of civic effort, there is also a lot more polarization and fragmentation and much less experience with everyday, practical problem solving across differences than there once was. People's organizations rooted in the life of communities—what can also be called free spaces or mediating institutions, like schools, political parties, locally grounded businesses, unions—once anchored citizenship in local communities. They sustained values of civic responsibility. They taught skills of engaging people who were different from immediate friends and family. They connected people's everyday life to the larger public world. Many of such mediating institutions have changed into service providers in recent decades. Instead of sites where people work together on everyday problems and develop habits and values of civic life, they now often simply provide services to clients and customers. This change has weakened civic muscle. It has contributed to the privatizing of our common world, the walling off of our imaginations and identities as well as our neighborhoods. Yet there are signs of change.

Something Is Stirring

"As the Constitutional Conventional of 1787 came to a close, after three and a half months of deliberation, a lady asked Dr. Franklin, 'Well, Doctor, what have we got, a republic or a monarchy?' 'A republic,' replied the Doctor. 'If you can keep it.'"[5]

Kelly Heskett, an undergraduate student at the University of Minnesota, related the pessimism she felt before taking a course called Organizing for the Public Good. "I've always felt like making a difference in the world could only be done if you were Oprah, Brad Pitt, or the president. Like a lot of people, I always felt powerless. I always waited for a super hero to be elected and change things."

Young adults like Heskett have grown up hearing news of mounting crises and global problems. They have also lived in a world of increasingly polarized, unproductive politics. They have learned little about intelligent, resourceful people like themselves who work together on collective challenges. From my interactions with hundreds of young people in our youth work at the Center for Democracy and Citizenship, I know that Heskett voiced the views of many in her generation when she concluded that powerful civic agents of change in the world are different than herself. But in the Organizing for the Public Good course, Heskett and others worked as teams to research people's organizations that citizens are creating or renewing, through which people act with power and effectiveness on public problems and issues. Then they developed messages that they thought their generation should hear.

Heskett, with two other students, investigated a group of parents in the southern suburbs of Minneapolis and St. Paul called Balance4-Success. She interviewed Andrea Grazzini Walstrom (whose story is told in more detail in Chapter 3), a leader in a group seeking to create balance in family life in a culture that is over-scheduled and corrosive of family time and community. Heskett and the other students decided that these problems are also present in young adults' lives. Heskett's experiences in the class expanded her sense of possibility. She became convinced that constructive change can occur and that she can be part of it. "I think something is stirring," she concluded. "Eventually this huge movement is going to take off. I can feel it."[6]

The civic leadership of visionary politicians is helpful — government is a resource that we certainly can't afford to ignore. But governments alone don't create community or produce powerful citizens or sustain the civic culture. As Benjamin Franklin realized, keeping the republic requires the efforts of millions of ordinary citizens. It also requires a new generation of people's organizations through which people develop public confidence, skills in dealing with others who are different, and power to take on the challenges facing our communities, our nation, and the world.

Recent years have seen a number of action-oriented books full of insights on successful grassroots civic action and institution building. Matt Leighninger detailed what can be gleaned from partnerships that have been developing between citizens and local governments in *The Next Form of Democracy: How Expert Rule Is Giving Way to Shared Governance*. Peter Levine described how young people are addressing public problems and showing signs that they may turn out to be a new civic generation in *The Future of Democracy*. Out of the partnership work at the Center for Democracy and Citizenship, Nan Kari and Nan Skelton's edited work *Voices of Hope: The Story of the Jane Addams School for Democracy* describes the decade-long work of building a community-based partnership for education, learning, and action between new immigrants and native-born Americans.

The Citizen Solution builds on these books and many others. I focus especially on the Twin Cities of Minneapolis and St. Paul, Minnesota, my home for more than thirty years, and the work of the Center for Democracy and Citizenship at the Humphrey Institute and that of our partners. We have long worked to identify and build methods and concepts that prepare citizens to be powerful agents of change and architects of their own lives.

The Citizen Solution is based on the belief that conversations, the everyday politics of public work, and civic learning can reverse negative trends and build a sustainable future. It is a story made up of many civic stories. It is also an invitation for all to join in the work of creating a multitude of new civic stories.

1 Working Together

The emerging civic movement changes the way we see citizens, professionals, government, and democracy itself. It teaches respect for the talents and intelligence of all men and women. It involves a renewed appreciation for places. All are necessary if we are to build civic agency, that is, the capacity to work with people of different political parties, faiths, races, incomes, ages, and cultures.

THE CITIZEN MOVEMENT IS BASED ON RENEWED RESPECT FOR the talents and intelligence of regular citizens. I participated in such a movement once before.

The civil rights movement that shaped me as a young man was full of faith in the capacities of people without degrees, formal credentials, or celebrity status—in this case, African Americans in the South, radically devalued by segregation. It was also full of leaders who illustrated the substance of this faith. Oliver Harvey, a janitor at Duke University where I went to college, organizer of a union of nonacademic employees for better pay and improved working conditions, was a great public intellectual and a mentor. He taught me about the black community, musical traditions, and decades-old struggles for civil rights.

For some time I worked for the Citizenship Education Program of the Southern Christian Leadership Conference (SCLC), the group headed by Martin Luther King. Although the citizenship efforts of SCLC are relatively invisible in most public histories of the movement, the program was crucial — Andrew Young once called it "the foundation of the whole movement." We organized citizenship schools, informal training in church basements, community centers, beauty parlors, and elsewhere that conveyed the skills of community action. Our message was simple: people have capacities to take self-reliant, cooperative, bold action. It was expressed in a song, "We Are the Ones We've Been Waiting For," sung by SCLC activist Dorothy Cotton, composed by Bernice Reagan, and inspired by a line in June Jordan's poem, "For South African Women." The song, in turn, inspired untold numbers of people.

I learned how the civil rights struggle was connected to earlier movements, when ordinary people were valued in the public culture and seen as the foundations of democracy. I had a dramatic experience of it in St. Augustine, Florida. One day I encountered a group of Ku Klux Klan members. I had gone out to the Old Jail because I was worried about a friend who had been arrested in a demonstration — the brutality that the jailors displayed toward civil rights demonstrators was a constant topic of conversation among SCLC staff members. Many people were held without water all day long, packed in an outdoor wire enclosure called "the pen." The hot Florida sun beat down relentlessly. Some passed out.

I talked to my friend, Cathy, through the bars. She was inside the jail and was fine. But when I came back to the car five men and a woman suddenly surrounded me. I realized that they must have followed me out from town. I was terrified. One said, "You're a goddamn Yankee communist. We're going to get you, boy."

I took a breath. Then my southern roots flooded back. I said, "I'm a Christian and the Bible says 'love your neighbor.' I love blacks, like I love whites. But I'm not a Yankee. My family has been in the South since before the Revolution. And I'm not a communist." Searching for a word to describe my confused identity—and remembering an occasional remark of my father—I tried on a different label. "I'm a populist," I said. "I believe that blacks and poor whites should get together and do something about the big shots who keep us divided and held down."

There was silence. The group looked at an older man, dressed in coveralls, wearing a straw hat, to see what he would say. He scratched his head. "There may be something in that," he said. "I don't know whether I'm populist. But I read about it. And I ain't stupid. The big shots look down on us. The mayor will congratulate us for beating you up. But he'd never talk to me on the street." He continued, "I ain't a Christian myself. I'm a Hinduist. I believe in the caste system." For a few minutes, we talked about what an interracial populist movement might look like. Then I drove quickly back into town.

Several days later the Ku Klux Klan held a march in front of the Southern Christian Leadership Conference office in the African American part of town. That summer was a battle of flags. Civil rights demonstrators marched under the American flag. The Klan countermarched under the Confederate flag.

I was standing with the crowd in front of the office, perhaps the only white in the group. Dr. King was nearby. The Klan philosopher, in the front row of their march, saw me and waved. I gave a tepid response, trying to be inconspicuous. But King saw my gesture. He asked me what that was all about. I told him the story. King said, "I've always identified with populism. That was a time when Negroes and whites found common ground." I had only a vague sense of what he meant— the term "populist" had floated into my consciousness like a rescue raft. But I learned more.

The original movement to go by the name populist formed in the 1880s and 1890s among black and white farmers in the South and Midwest. It included interracial alliances that defied racial taboos. Black historian Manning Marable recounts his family's story about his great-grandfather: "During the 1880s, many black and white farmers in Alabama joined the Alliance, a radical agrarian movement against the conservative business and planter elite. Morris was attracted to the movement because of its racial egalitarianism. Throughout Georgia and Alabama, black and white Populist Party members held joint picnics, rallies, and speeches. Populist candidate Reuben F. Kalb actually won the state gubernatorial contest in 1894 [though electoral fraud prevented his taking office]. On the periphery of this activity, in his small rural town, Morris Marable became sheriff with the support of blacks and whites. He was intensely proud of his office, and completed his duties with special dispatch."[1]

King obviously knew about populism's interracial history. He assigned me to organize poor whites. He also told me that he believed the next stage of the movement would need to address issues of economic injustice and poverty across racial lines. Soon after, on a dusty road in the black community of St. Augustine, I decided that my life work would be helping to organize a democratic movement bringing together blacks and whites, people whose talents had been undervalued all their lives, in order to build a better society. I believe we are on the threshold of such a movement in Minnesota, in the nation, and in fact around the world.

A Paradigm Shift

Civic respect implies a change in paradigm to what we at the Center for Democracy and Citizenship (CDC) call the public-work framework for action. The CDC defines public work as sustained, visible effort by a mix of people that creates things — material or cultural — of lasting civic impact, while developing civic learning and capacity in the process.

Public work shifts from the paradigm that now dominates in most professional systems and in many institutions, a paradigm centered around one-way expert interventions, to a citizen-centered approach that is based on the need for strong civic agency. The public-work framework liberates professionals, expanding their power and effectiveness as they give up the illusion that they can—or should—control processes and outcomes. This change in paradigm is necessary for the kind of exponential increase in effective public actions required to address our common challenges in communities and the world.

The shift that is needed entails changes in how we understand citizens and citizenship, the role of professionals, the nature of government, and the meaning of democracy. It means a move from seeing most citizens as voters, volunteers, clients, consumers, or aggrieved and powerless outsiders to seeing all people as potential problem solvers and co-creators of public goods. It involves a shift in the role of professionals, including civil servants, nonprofit managers, teachers, health providers, clergy, and elected office-holders, from being providers of services and expert solutions to being partners, educators, and organizers of cooperative action. Overall, it entails a change in the framework of the meaning of democracy, shifting from a focus on elections to a focus on democratic society. It involves shifting from reliance on groups of experts to broad collaborations that tap diverse energies and skills.

In a democratic society, government is not outside the realm of our common life, and citizens do not exist in a separate arena called "civil society." Rather, government is a catalyst and resource of communities and citizens, helping create environments that energize and equip people to be the navigators of their own lives and communities in open environments where there are no predetermined outcomes. This paradigm renews government "of the people and by the people," not simply "for the people," to recall Abraham Lincoln's great formulation. It recognizes that civil servants are themselves citizens, doing the people's work. Government can generate leadership, resources, tools, and rules. But officials are not the center of the civic universe, nor is government the only location for democracy. Democracy is a way of life rooted in living communities; it is a work in progress.

This shift from government-centered democracy to citizen-centered democracy and civic agency will transform people's sense of possibilities. Today most people feel overwhelmed about mounting challenges, from global warming to poverty, from achievement gaps to providing health care and creating healthy communities. The public-work paradigm can renew hope that we can address such problems effectively and even that such challenges are opportunities for growth. Over time the paradigm of democratic society as the public work of all citizens will create a culture of abundance, as well as a more cooperative society. Individualism and personal success are important American traits, but this culture has gotten out of whack. We need to move to a balance between the individual and the community — to shift from me to we.

Other nations' perspectives can help us conceptualize the paradigm shift. A chart by Marie Ström, of the Institute for Democracy in South Africa, a public-interest organization that works with communities across Africa, shows how questions would be answered very differently in a society based on cooperative public work.[2]

Shifting from a focus on government and experts to a focus on the whole citizenry will not be simple or easy. Such a shift challenges dominant trends in the twentieth century that have devalued the talents and intelligence of people without credentials, degrees, and titles. The civil rights movement of the late 1950s and 1960s, with its respect for the talents of those Dr. King called "unlettered men and women," was going against the grain. The shift also counters cultural, economic, and social forces in the globalizing world that put local communities under siege. This shift depends on two dynamics: the return of the people to public life and a renewed appreciation for local communities as the root system of democracy.

The People in Public Life

In May 1997, I was in Washington for a meeting of the National Commission for Civic Renewal. The commission was a bipartisan group that

TABLE 1

HOW PUBLIC PARTICIPATION DIFFERS FROM CITIZEN AGENCY

	PUBLIC PARTICIPATION Government consults citizens to learn their views	CITIZEN AGENCY Citizens shape their own lives and communities
Definition of democracy	Democratic state with free elections	Democratic society created by citizens' ongoing work
Basic question	What can government do?	What can we all do?
Who is in control?	Government, whose leaders are not everyday citizens	Citizens, including citizens inside government
Who initiates?	Government	Citizens and their government (acting as catalyst and resource)
What is the outcome?	Customer service: People consulted. Government takes note. Services delivered.	Creation of the commonwealth: Public problems solved. Public wealth created. Civic capacity and democratic culture developed.
What is the attitude?	Condescension by government and dependency by citizenry	Respect for the capacities and resourcefulness of citizens
What is the pattern of interaction between citizens and government?	Consumer attitude: complaint, protest, dog-eat-dog competition	Producer attitude: partnerships, negotiations, ownership, co-learning
How realistic is it?	Seems realistic, but in fact is more idealized. Most problems are too big for government alone to handle.	Seems naïve, but in fact is more realistic and promising. Recognizes that the people are a key, largely untapped resource.
What are elections about?	Which candidate can fix things	What leader works best with citizens
What is the philosophy?	Public and private scarcity	Democratic abundance

Marie Ström, Institute for Democracy in South Africa, 2007

documented the decline of many forms of civic involvement—voting levels, membership in service associations organizations, and trust in public institutions. The commission was also exploring early signs of the new citizen movement that is now gathering momentum a decade later.

One morning I went to an exhibit called *A New Deal for the Arts* at the National Archives Building on Constitution Avenue. The exhibit featured public artwork from the Great Depression of the 1930s and the broad political and social movement called the New Deal.

During the New Deal, federal arts programs employed thousands of writers, sculptors, musicians, photographers, painters, and other cultural workers, and public-works programs not only provided jobs but helped to counteract the cultural gloom of the Great Depression. The exhibit represented many styles and a vast array of approaches, cultures, and traditions. African American theater posters from Harlem were on display. So were works of eastern European cabinetmakers and great photojournalists. The exhibit also showed political posters and the works of regionalist artists and socialist realists.

The exhibit showed how widespread the public-works arts movement was, what it meant to those involved, and the powerful messages it conveyed to society. The movement involved millions of citizens in different ways, such as art classes and community-debated mural designs for two thousand post offices. The great composer Aaron Copeland tried out his compositions before local audiences to get feedback before he made them final.

New Deal cultural work challenged the dominant elitist views of the time. Cultural workers focused on the dignity, energy, and work of common men and women in the midst of hardship and their contributions to pressing challenges such as hunger or soil conservation during the Dust Bowl years. New Deal artists often had controversial views, and their works were challenged, debated, and discussed in communities. But the overall impression I took from the exhibit was the strength of artists' sense of their public mission. They embraced subjects that were native, understandable, and meaningful to most Americans and emphasized themes such as work, community, and democracy. Overall, the exhibit opened a window for me into the consciousness of professional artists who saw themselves as a part of the life of the people. As social critic Lewis Mumford observed, "Artists have been given something more precious than their daily bread . . . the knowledge that their work has a destination in the community."[3]

I left the National Archives thinking about how "the people," seen by intellectuals in the 1920s as the repository of crass materialism and parochialism, had been rediscovered as a source of strength and hope by many intellectuals, professionals, and political leaders in the 1930s. "The heart and soul of our country," Franklin Roosevelt said in 1940, "is the heart and soul of the common man." This spirit helped to shape the civil rights movement, and many architects of the movement like Ella Baker, Bayard Rustin, Stanley Levison, and A. Philip Randolph had roots in the New Deal.

After the civil rights era, public respect for ordinary people's talents declined. I saw an example of this erosion when I left the National Archives and went to the newly opened Franklin Delano Roosevelt Memorial, which is made up of seven acres of open sculptural rooms that depict the New Deal period. The memorial, along the Tidal Basin, is beautifully landscaped, and it displays the considerable architectural talents of the designer, Lawrence Halprin. The team of five sculptors he assembled included many leading figures in contemporary public art. Among the group was George Segal, often called "the sculptor of the common man and woman." While other sculptures depict Franklin and Eleanor Roosevelt, Segal's two sculptures feature ordinary citizens. In *Rural Couple*, a woman sits on a rocking chair with a man standing beside her. It suggests a farm scene, perhaps on a front porch. Nearby, the sculpture *The Breadline* portrays citizens in an urban environment. Both embody Segal's longstanding emphasis on human emotions and everyday experiences.

In both statues the citizens are drained of energy. Their faces are vacant; their posture droops. They seem to be anonymous and miserable "masses." This version of New Deal history contrasted radically with the images I had seen in the New Deal artworks themselves, whose energy helped to end the Depression. The Roosevelt memorial offers the message that Roosevelt saved a victimized and helpless people, and Halprin confirmed that he wanted to highlight how FDR "faced challenges and was able to effect solutions." The memorial also makes a broader statement about educated elites seeing their role as rescuing people.

This role is not malevolent. Quite the contrary, it is infused with good intentions. Similarly, when I talk with students about the possibility that their efforts to help the poor and oppressed might disempower people, their first reaction is disbelief. But I am convinced that such disempowerment often happens through professional "rescue" that erodes people's sense of their own powers and capacities. This "rescue from above" explains much of the powerlessness that many people feel and is also a reason for weakened communities. The concept also illuminates the burn-out felt by professionals who feel called to save others or solve problems by themselves.

Powerlessness and Expert Control

Many diagnoses are offered to explain the erosion of community life and social ties that scholars have documented: growing inequalities, unraveling public morality, problems in the formal political system, and consumerist culture. All play a role. But from a perspective that focuses on civic agency—the powers of ordinary people to be agents and architects of their own lives and to work together on common challenges—the elephant in the room, the cause behind the cause, is the widespread sense of powerlessness and fragmentation. This is caused

by the weakening of the values, ties, knowledge, and skills that are essential for common work.

In 1996, the Kettering Foundation commissioned the Harwood
Group, a public-issues research firm, to conduct focus groups across the
country in order to understand "the nature and extent of the disconnect
between what people see as important concerns and their sense that they
can address them." The focus groups discovered a nation of citizens
deeply troubled about the direction of the society as a whole, even if
they felt optimistic about their own personal lives and economic
prospects. They saw large institutions, from government to business to
education, as increasingly remote and focused on narrow gain. They
worried that America is becoming a greedy nation, where looking out
for number one and getting rich quick replaces hard work, accountability, community and family life, and a sense of the human and the sacred.
Focus group participants expressed grave concerns that people are increasingly divided by race, ideology, religion, and class. Society used to
"build walls to put the bad people in," said one man in Memphis. "Now
we're building walls to keep the bad people out," something he saw as
futile. "There's no sense of community anymore. Everybody is walled
off from the other neighborhood."

Participants also said they felt powerless to do much about these
trends. As a result they found themselves retreating into smaller and
smaller circles of private life where they felt some control, even if they
thought that retreat spelled trouble. "If you look at the whole picture of
everything that is wrong, it is so overwhelming," said one woman from
Richmond, Virginia. She voiced widely held sentiments. "You just retreat back and take care of what you know you can take care of — and
you make it smaller, make it even down to just you and your unit. You
know you can take care of that."[4]

A parallel study of baby boomers and older adults in 1999 by the
Minnesota Board of Aging found similar results. Both baby boomers
and older adults expressed a strong desire to feel useful, to make serious

contributions to rebuilding a sense of community, and to be involved in decision making about the shape of their communities. Citizens wanted to learn civic skills such as how to work across common social divisions of ideology, race, or culture and how to think about the bigger picture that ties tasks to larger questions.

Citizens also thought that most volunteer opportunities, while important, relegated them to "positions of mediocrity with the assumption that they lack the capacity to work on big issues that impact the community." Volunteers, in their view, were rarely asked "what they are good at, what is important to them, and how they want to be part of shaping their communities."[5]

Condescension toward volunteers derives from what can be called technocracy, a mode of domination that has spread throughout our society like a silent civic disease. Technocracy means control by experts who see themselves outside a common civic life, whose authority comes from book learning and formal credentials and whose superiority is based on supposedly objective and scientific knowledge. Technocracy turns groups of people into abstract categories. It strips issues away from the context of the communities where they occur. It creates silo, or isolating, cultures in institutions based on specialized identities, languages, and ways of working. It radically erodes respect for citizens.

Joan Didion detailed the consequences of domination by experts in her book *Political Fictions*, based on her essays in the *New York Review of Books* on presidential campaigns from 1988 to 2000. Among most Democratic candidates and their staffs, she found a vivid assumption of superiority. "I recall pink-cheeked young aides on the Dukakis campaign referring to themselves, innocent of irony and so of history, as 'the best and the brightest,'" she writes. Conservative politicians were equally arrogant.[6]

Developments in higher education in the last half century or so help explain the condescension that Didion found in the American political class. A 1989 lecture at the University of Illinois by Donna Shalala, then chancellor of the University of Wisconsin, later secretary of health and human services under President Clinton, illustrated the conviction that higher education's role is to train experts who will fix problems and people. Shalala made an impassioned plea for public service and social justice, for struggles against racism and sexism, for environmentalism and peace. She called for public universities to engage the world. Her good intentions were palpable. And they were also tied explicitly to technocracy. For her, "the ideal [is] a disinterested technocratic elite" fired by the moral mission of "society's best and brightest in service to its most needy." The imperative was "delivering the miracles of social science" to fix society's problems "just as doctors cured juvenile rickets in the past."[7] In this framework, most people have little to do except to give thanks or to complain if they don't like the cure.

The belief that most people are deficient and that universities train elites to save people and solve society's problems is crackpot conventional wisdom. "Access Versus Excellence" was how Minnesota Public Radio framed its statewide discussion in 2001 on the future of the University of Minnesota. It took as self-evident that large numbers of students of diverse backgrounds would mean a decline in standards of excellence.

But signs of the return of the people — recognition of ordinary people's capacities and talents — are also emerging in the United States and around the world. Such recognition calls for a new kind of professional, able to work as a catalyst, organizer, and educator. The awarding of the 2006 Nobel Peace Prize to Muhammad Yunus for his pioneering work in micro-lending in Bangladesh and elsewhere is a case in point. Yunus's concept of micro-lending combines tremendous knowledge and craft with a deep respect for the capacities of poor people, especially poor women, to become agents of their own development and co-creators of their communities.

Important developments in higher education are also bucking the trend. The American Association of State Colleges and Universities

(AASCU)—a group representing America's local and regional higher education institutions, including Winona State, Metropolitan State, and Minneapolis Community and Technical College—has developed an explicit philosophical commitment to become "stewards of place." In 2008, the Center for Democracy and Citizenship began to work with AASCU on a long-range project to put a focus on civic agency at the center of these schools. "AASCU institutions are ideal places to focus on building the capacity for civic agency among students, faculty, and staff," argues George Mehaffy, AASCU vice president for leadership. "They are a laboratory for democracy." Mehaffy's conviction about AASCU institutions as promising settings for civic agency grows out of his experiences in directing AASCU's American Democracy Project (ADP), a civic-engagement initiative now involving 228 colleges and universities that is focused on higher education's role in preparing the next generation of citizens. That project, created in 2003, began with a call for campus participation; within a month, 135 institutions had signed up, and many more have joined since.

The ADP has spawned an array of projects and activities, national conferences, a Wingspread report, tens of thousands of entries on the Internet, and two national initiatives—the Political Engagement and the Stewardship of Public Lands projects. In both, campuses stress the roles and responsibilities of ordinary citizens and emphasize the development of political skills.[8]

Like the leaders of the ADP, few people in America really believe that experts by themselves have the wisdom or skill to solve complex problems. Just as intellectuals in the Eastern bloc once sounded the death knell of communism, Americans need to put an end to an outdated philosophy of expert rule in which few believe, but which still tends to hold us all in thrall.[9] Technocracy cannot be overcome simply by criticizing it. We need an alternative, a positive intellectual and practical project for the twenty-first century. I am convinced that building civic agency, our abilities to be the agents and architects of our own lives and to work together across differences on common problems and tasks, is the great challenge we face. Developing civic agency means recognizing diverse talents. It also calls for renewed appreciation for local communities in which people live and work as the root system of democracy.

The Return of Place

Most institutions of higher education once saw their work as developing citizens of actual places. The late Hubert H. Humphrey, for example, traced his famous political career back to his father's drugstore in Doland, South Dakota, in his autobiography, *The Education of a Public Man.*[10] The drugstore was a free space. "In his store there was eager talk about politics, town affairs, and religion," Humphrey wrote. "I've listened to some of the great parliamentary debates of our time, but have seldom heard better discussions of basic issues than I did as a boy standing on a wooden platform behind the soda fountain."

The drugstore created an all-partisan root system for democracy, schooling the father and the son in skills of political engagement. Humphrey's father was one of a handful of Democrats in a town with hundreds of Republicans. "Dad was a Democrat among friends and neighbors who took their Republicanism—along with their religion—very seriously." His father became the highly regarded mayor of the town.

The store functioned as a local lending library and cultural center—music came from the window of the second floor, from his father's rickety phonograph. It embodied a rich conception of civic agency and democracy as a way of life built through citizen labors. "[As] a druggist in a tiny town in the middle of the continent, American history and world affairs were as real to him as they were in Washington," wrote Humphrey. "Time after time, when he read about some political development . . . he'd say, 'You should know this, Hubert. It might affect your life someday.'" The store was a setting where people from the community also talked about problems and often decided to take action.[11]

The drugstore was a free space because his father saw himself as a citizen pharmacist and civic businessman of Doland. The chapter title in Humphrey's book makes the point, "Never a Pill without an Idea." His father worked in public ways. He championed public goods. He organized other citizens and learned from them, while improving the civic culture. He mentored his son.

All these elements wove through the illustrious career of Hubert H. Humphrey. Humphrey challenged and educated his audiences in ways that pointed to the complex interactions between the citizens working in government and other citizens. "Government isn't supposed to do all of this," he said during a February 22, 1967, television interview, in response to a caller who asked him to fix the problems with politics. "If you think politics is corrupt, get your bar of political Ivory soap and clean it up. Get out there and get roughed up a little bit in the world of reality.[12]

Civic professionals like Humphrey were once numerous. They could be found sustaining not only drugstores but also other free spaces like religious congregations, unions, ethnic organizations, settlement houses, neighborhood schools, colleges, Cooperative Extension, and many other settings. I saw them in the civil rights movement in black churches and in beauty parlors. Such free spaces were anchoring structures where people learned the basic skills and values of dealing with different sorts of people — negotiation, discussion, navigating the messy, open-ended ambiguity of public life. They were also environments in which people experienced power and creativity through public life. While these organizations had parochial elements, they also could form seedbeds for great movements like the New Deal and civil rights.

Some examples of civic professionals continue. For instance, Tom Gupta carries on the tradition of civic pharmacist that he heard about from Humphrey at the University of Minnesota, as a young student from India in the 1960s. His Scheider's Drug Store on University Avenue in Minneapolis continues to function as a lively center of civic discussion and neighborhood life. But most professionals have lost their connection to places. As they did so they came to identify far more with other professionals in their fields than with fellow citizens of their communities. The result has been what Thomas Bender calls a shift from "civic professionalism" to "disciplinary professionalism."[13]

Professional education has played a major role in this process. In seminaries and divinity schools, according to Mary Fulkerson, a professor at Duke Divinity School who studies theological education, the "practice courses" typically pertain to matters internal to the life of a congregation, such as preaching, counseling, and church organization. The skills, knowledge, and habits needed to engage with places where congregations are located are missing. Similarly, studies by the Center for School Change at the Humphrey Institute have found that teacher-education curriculum typically includes little or nothing on learning to work collaboratively with parents and other stakeholders.[14]

When such learning is absent, graduates come to understand themselves as detached experts providing service *for* people, not as citizens working *with* fellow citizens on public problems ranging from the education of young people to sustainable local development and global warming. Today, public commentators reinforce the idea that professionals are high-achieving strivers who have little identification with places. "Elites are cosmopolitan; people are local," as the sociologist Manuel Castells expressed conventional wisdom. New cosmopolitans are understood to be the upwardly mobile knowledge workers, at home in the global economy, individualistic, committed to diversity, detached from identities of locality, ethnicity, religion, or American society.[15]

But under the surface, a countertrend has been developing that helps to explain the new citizen movement. A bridging group that might be called local cosmopolitans has developed, many of them professionals who have reconnected to places. They value diversity and pluralism, but they also have strong roots in local communities. Since the 1970s, they have been expanding in numbers and creating new institutions.

Local cosmopolitans first appeared as the baby boomers grew older. Jim Gambone and Erica Whittlinger argue that the baby-boom generation has been largely misrepresented as being concerned only with individual self-realization. In fact, they were influenced by 1960s values such as participatory democracy and community as well as individual expression. As boomers had children, bought homes, and built local bridging structures, they deepened their roots. Their efforts fed into the 1970s neighborhood movement, what the *Christian Science Monitor* called the "invisible story of the decade."[16]

In subsequent decades, local cosmopolitans generated a multitude of civic experiments, countertrends to declines in traditional service groups and also to the polarization of America into red versus blue states. Their efforts include land trusts and watershed groups, community arts efforts, farmers' markets, libraries and local schools with community orientations, and a robust movement to create lively, vital public spaces of many other kinds.[17] They also include large initiatives like the American Democracy Project of the American Association of State Colleges and Universities. All these efforts bring people together despite religious, ethnic, economic, partisan, and other differences. They generate conversations and public work based on diversity, and local cultures based on equal respect.

Several trends feed local cosmopolitanism. Gar Alperovitz and his colleagues in the project Community Wealth have documented place-enhancing economic developments. While manufacturing jobs have declined, locally based service jobs have mushroomed to more than 80 percent of the workforce. With its locally rooted service jobs, America is the least globalized of all the major economies. Place-based economic activity like employee-owned businesses, municipally owned enterprises, community development corporations, and for-profit activity by nonprofits generates community wealth, not simply private riches. All confound partisan divides. Thus, the supposedly conservative state of Alabama aggressively promotes worker-owned companies with pension funds.[18]

In Minnesota, such new civic trends are strong. The Citizens League, a group at the center of the civic landscape, illustrates all of them. It has been revitalized since Sean Kershaw became director in 2003 and helped to shift its framework to focus on how citizens are developed.

The Citizens League was created in 1952 by leading professionals and businessmen in Minneapolis as a nonpartisan public policy group, "dedicated to the common good" beyond parochial or partisan interests. The Citizens League, an organization with individual members, has long been an architect of public policy in the state and is often a leader in national policy innovation. The group helped to create a metropolitan parks system, to reorganize hospital care, and to found the Metropolitan Regional Council, a body that has led the nation in thinking about regional approaches to problems such as transportation, environmental protection, and affordable housing. The Citizens League proposed successful reforms of state financial aid to schools and cities. Such leadership led *Time* magazine, in a famous 1973 cover story on the Minnesota Miracle, to single out the Citizens League as the state's most notable civic force.[19]

The Citizens League has made major contributions to the large-scale systems infrastructure (detailed in Chapter 4). But it also embodied the technocratic temper of the times. "The League has been both an architect and a reflection of the civic culture," said Kershaw. "In the early decades this meant our style was mainly set by experts who had a civic side. Our policy success had to do with the civic culture in Minnesota. But we were also victims of the expert-dominated approach."[20]

In practice, through the 1970s and 1980s the Citizens League focused on efficiency and better service. A 1971 report, "Why Not Buy Service?" set the trend for the next three decades with its recommendation that "government should buy results." Once again, the Citizens League helped to establish a national pattern, one that informed the reinventing government initiative during the Clinton administration. This had positive features in reorienting civil servants outward, toward the needs of diverse groups. But it had a very large flaw: citizens were redefined as customers (see Chapter 10 for ideas about how to change the customer mindset).

By the late 1990s, the limits of focusing on efficient service delivery were becoming clear to some in the Citizens League, as it experienced declining membership and energy. In response, the league undertook a major strategic study in 2002 called the Common Good Better. Leaders held conversations with citizens from various backgrounds. Their report called for a major shift toward rebuilding the civic infrastructure. Again there are parallels in the Clinton administration, which worked with the Humphrey Center's bipartisan New Citizenship coalition, using the theme that "we can't reinvent government without reinventing citizenship."

The Citizens League shifted from the white-paper approach that had characterized much of its history to a focus on civic capacity building. Kershaw sees this as partly a generational shift, expressing the desire of young adults today to be co-creators of the world they live in. It also recalled older themes. Kershaw came from a family with roots in the 1930s. His father, from a family farm in Nebraska, had experienced both the poverty of the Great Depression and also its civic energies. His parents both had strong commitments to civic life. Kershaw described his father as "one of the last real family physicians, the opposite of the expert doctor, a citizen professional." He made house calls and also helped organize an environmental effort to create a public land trust. Kershaw, growing up "in the background of all this civic activity," developed a passion for public life, which he never saw as partisan politics.

In the 1990s, Kershaw helped organize Active Citizenship, a group of young professionals in the Twin Cities that adapted public achievement concepts and methods of everyday politics (described in Chapter 7).

"We wanted to counter the cynicism of so many in our generation, the sense that nothing could be done about public problems. We also realized we needed to move beyond the charity approach. Our real interest was in having meaningful work that makes a public contribution." Kershaw was active in the Citizens League Common Good study. After working for St. Paul city government, he became the Citizens League's youngest executive director. The organization has changed significantly. Its first principle declares, "We believe in the power and potential of all citizens," arguing that "all Minnesotans are capable of developing an in-depth understanding of complicated public problems. . . . This capacity must be developed and encouraged." The Citizens League is attracting younger members — more than half of new memberships are people under age forty. Partly in response, the league has created ways for people to have fun while being involved in public conversations and action, such as the popular and lively Policy and a Pint evening discussions.

The league also created a Minnesota anniversary project, MAP 150. It marks the state's sesquicentennial celebration in 2008 with a challenge to expert domination. "When citizens are co-producers of the public good, policies will look different and outcomes for the common good will improve," reads its statement. "Policy is now primarily set by experts and vested interests, which leads to excessive partisanship, gridlock, and policy stagnation. . . . The goal of MAP 150 is to reinvent policymaking by reconnecting the vision, values, and voices of Minnesotans with policymaking."[21] The focus on civic capacity building has changed the Citizens League's own approach to policymaking. "For instance, last year we decided to take action on mental health," Kershaw says. "Traditionally this would have meant doing more white papers. But mental health has been white-papered to death. So we convened many different interests and groups — providers, advocates, legislators, and others. Many hated each other. But we learned how to work together." As a result, the Minnesota legislature in 2007 passed the first new funding for mental health initiatives in many years, with bipartisan support.

Sean Kershaw, like Kelly Heskett, sees something stirring among young people. "Young people are not apathetic or narcissistic. They want to be civically involved," he said. "But they don't oppose self-interests to civic involvement. They don't think that the big institutions are working too well. And they often feel powerless." The new energy and innovations of the Citizens League illustrate civic ferment in Minnesota and build on core values and themes in our heritage.

First Civic Skill: One-On-One Interviews

A one-on-one interview is an intentional process of getting to know what motivates another person. It helps to develop respect for people of different backgrounds and is the foundation for work across differences. Some call the one-on-one the genius of the new generation of civic efforts because it breaks down stereotypes, and it also changes the rules of involvement. Today, much activism is based on the idea of "outreach," trying to get people involved in the issues that have already been defined, directed toward outcomes already determined. If you use one-on-ones to discover other people's self-interests and build on them in serious ways, you are doing something different: enlisting people by engaging them in what they are interested in. You begin to co-create the civic effort together.

A one-on-one involves a conscious exploration of another person's interests, passions, most important relationships, and stories. One-on-ones depend on putting aside prejudgments and stereotypes and listening carefully and strategically. If you do this much, people will constantly surprise and sometimes amaze you with talents and insights you never imagined. One-on-one interviews are also a way to develop new power through building public relationships across lines of difference. Like other civic skills, they involve a good deal of practice.

To find out others' self-interests requires that you learn to listen in a particular way, with attention to body language, emotional tone, perhaps a sparkle in the eye. You identify what energizes and activates the other person. One-on-ones aim at "public knowledge"—you are listening for people's public interests and potential to take action with others. You are not creating a therapeutic or intimate relationship, where you delve into hardships in order to provide comfort.

TIPS AND TOOLS

Be prepared: It is best to set up interviews in advance, think about what you want to know, and make the interview short (at least the initial one), about a half hour.

Keep it informal: A one-on-one interview differs from a job interview, a survey, or an academic interview. You do not proceed with a standardized set of questions—you go with the flow, looking for body language, sources of passion, personal histories.

Look for connections: Ask questions to keep the conversation flowing. Look for connections and contrasts in experience between yourself and your interviewee, but resist launching into long stories about yourself. The other person should be doing most of the talking.

Ask direct questions: Find out what is important to the other person. For instance, ask about her connections to her home, or how she came to her job. Find out about the public issues that make her angry or energized. "Why did you get involved in this group?" "Why do you care about this issue?" "What have you learned from this experience?"

Avoid asking yes and no questions: They are too quick and you don't learn much. If you do ask them, follow up with "why?"

Listen well: Build on what your interviewee has already said. This involves paying close attention. An interviewee who feels listened to is likely to talk more than someone who feels that their words are falling on deaf ears.

Be sure you understand: Clarify what the talker is saying by restating what you've heard and asking if you've got it right.

Look for the energy for action: If you can see that the person is fired up about a public problem, ask if she has ever taken action on it before and how. Find out if she would be interested in working with others to take further action. Plan a follow-up meeting, if it is useful.

Evaluate: Afterward, think about the outcome of the interview. What worked? What can you do better next time?[22]

2 Minnesota's Living Civic Culture

Garrison Keillor's writings and radio broadcast, *Prairie Home Companion*, have popularized Minnesota's distinctive civic culture. At its heart are these key elements: that people make their culture, rather than just having it handed down to them, and that public problem solving builds our communities' capacity for working together. Two stories illustrate these elements returning in the twenty-first century.

"Minnesota's distinctiveness [is] the result of an unusually vibrant civic culture, one in which citizens engage in widespread discourse and action on matters of common interest."[1]

NINA ARCHABAL, DIRECTOR OF THE MINNESOTA HISTORICAL SOCIETY

WHEN THE I-35 BRIDGE OVER THE MISSISSIPPI RIVER in Minneapolis collapsed on August 1, 2007, people around the world were riveted by scenes of the spectacular disaster. They were also struck by something else: the amazing outpouring of volunteer and professional citizen energies. Hundreds of people in passing cars stopped to help. Many jumped into the river to rescue survivors. Others consoled victims. Rescue workers from the nearby University of Minnesota appeared within moments.

Dave Scharnhorst's car was on the bridge when it went down, but he was able to drive off and park. He headed back to help and found a woman shaking. "I got to talk with her and calm her down, which coincidently was calming me down," he explained. "I had to have something to do." In the days following, thousands of people volunteered. More than 20,000 meals were served to first responders. More than 2,500 people donated blood. "Minneapolis Shows Why It's Rated Number One in Volunteerism," read a news headline the next week.[2]

Citizens anywhere commonly respond to disasters either by voluntary efforts or by professional emergency-response work. But the outpouring in Minnesota was remarkable. It reflected a vibrant civic heritage and culture created by citizens of different religious, cultural, ethnic, and income backgrounds who worked, often across differences, to solve problems. Minnesota has, in fact, pioneered in civic involvement by businesses and unions, stewardship of natural resources, community support for the arts, family farm protection, and community-centered educational innovations. Minneapolis enacted the first enforceable fair employment legislation against racial discrimination of any city in the nation. Minnesota has the highest voting level in the United States; the Twin Cities has the highest percentage of volunteers.

Insightful leaders have never taken the civic culture for granted. As former governor Elmer L. Andersen put it at the groundbreaking for the Minnesota History Center in 1988, "Our future depends on our ability to preserve and transmit the rich heritage. But we cannot assume it will be automatically adopted by future generations."[3]

Two stories illustrate the process of civic renewal after civic decline. Though they take place in different settings and address different issues, both tackle twenty-first-century challenges using old Minnesota themes of community building and of making our civic culture.

Global Warming

Minnesota's wave of new activism on climate change and related issues like energy independence reflects the Minnesota sense that, as Ted Kolderie, former director of the Citizens League, put it, what is distinctive about the quality of the state is that "this place is made."[4] This open, co-created sense of culture combines with a concern about global warming that crosses political divides. "Environmental issues, especially at state and local levels, are bringing together conservatives and liberals who agree on little else. . . in a polarized nation," wrote Paul Nussbaum for the *Philadelphia Inquirer* in 2005.[5]

Concern about climate change across the globe might well prove a profound catalyst for civic engagement everywhere. This is because action to reduce carbon emissions, to take other measures to reverse global warming, and to instill a deeper ethic of stewardship and conservation will not happen without changes in a myriad of everyday practices, cultural values, and civic institutions, ranging from our families and neighborhoods to our colleges and universities. Such changes require citizen action on a large scale.

These ideas infuse the thinking of Timothy DenHerder-Thomas, who decided to go to Macalester College in St. Paul in 2005, the same spring that Nussbaum wrote about the new environmentalism. Tim was born in Bahrain — his father's family is Indian, his mother's is Dutch from Minnesota — and he grew up in Jersey City, New Jersey. He had been concerned about the environment from an early age and had also been frustrated by attitudes in his low-income community. "People didn't have a very strong sense of the neighborhood," he said. "And they tended to think of themselves as consumers of society." He was also discontented with the fatalism he saw among many young people. "Young people feel they don't have agency. Things just happen. Society just runs. You have to fit in, whether it's a job that you don't like or sitting in traffic. They just think it's the way things are rather than we have a role and the ability to change things."[6]

When he visited Macalester on a college tour he liked the academic excellence and also the international atmosphere. But a more intangible quality especially appealed to him. "Minnesota seemed to me like an active community. People actually treat things as if they can shape them, rather than just react." He also felt that there was a need to take action as a young person. "The renewable energy movement in Minnesota is very developed, but when I got here, statewide youth organizing wasn't there."

Tim enrolled in Macalester after a summer experience with the Climate Campaign in Boston, a youth-run organization that was working on global warming campaigns, had deepened his sense of civic possibility. "It was amazing. They were talking about how young people across the country are building campus efforts and working with even larger-scale efforts. It gave me a sense of what is needed — instead of arguing for changes, young people are actually demonstrating that they can happen."

At Macalester, he joined with a group, MacCARES (the Macalester Conservation and Renewable Energy Society). He worked to do a preliminary carbon inventory of the campus, to find out how much carbon different buildings were emitting through electric usage and heating. It turned out that a lot of buildings were hotter than they needed to be, and the students found many staff in facilities management were sympathetic to making changes. This effort quickly integrated with many others — student analysis of dorm efficiency, a project to design a roof system that would literally be green, involving roofs covered with plants in shallow soil. "Green roofs," as they are called, reduce overall heat from the city, reduce runoff, improve insulation, and also bring green space to the campus. The students got backing from the city of St. Paul, and also companies like American Hydrotech and Greenroof Block that are involved in green roofing.

In the spring of 2006 Tim helped organize one of the first student-initiated Clean Energy Revolving Funds in the nation. "Students usually raise money for an environmental project, do it, and then are back to square one, starting over. We wanted to create a way to cycle funds to provide new funds for new projects over a long period of time." Harvard had a fund that got returns on investment of up to 30 percent for projects like community-based wind turbines. The idea caught on at Macalester, with an initial $27,000 of support from student government and the environmental studies department. They had decided not to initially ask for funding from the administration, where the project would go through a long review, though students communicated regularly with administrators. After the idea gathered student and faculty support, Macalester president Brian Rosenberg allocated another $40,000 in the fall of 2006. The project, called CERF, or Clean Energy Revolving Fund, reflects Tim's philosophy — the challenges of global climate change need to be reconceived as an opportunity. "I don't talk about conservation, which implies sacrifice," he said. "It's not as positive as smart energy lifestyles. I think the environmental challenge presents us with opportunities to reunite communities and to create culture change. It can be incredibly beneficial."

Significantly, Tim sees the new climate change movement as about power. "We talk about people power, and how this work allows anyone to take part. It's about local solutions, and of course about energy itself—powering our society. If government tried to mandate the changes that we need by itself, there would be riots." Tim and other students wanted their work to connect to the larger community, so they made connections with small businesses, religious groups, labor unions, people involved in rural development, and high school students to create a network called the World Energy Community Action Network. "WeCAN is the name," Tim explained, "because we want to change people's thinking that it's not realistic to make big changes. WeCAN affirms that all of us have a role in determining what a sustainable society will look like. The WeCAN idea is that it keeps growing. It's about citizen empowerment, people determining the shape of their futures. It's not accepting the assumption that global warming is not our responsibility. Politicians can't do this for us. But we all can do it together."

Returning Veterans

The Warrior to Citizen campaign addresses a much different question but it also ties action on an issue to community building and culture change in communities and people's organizations. It began in the fall of 2006, when a group of four mid-career professionals in the Humphrey Institute Policy Fellows leadership program chose to work on veterans' issues. They anticipated the return of 2,600 members of the Minnesota Army National Guard in the summer of 2007, and decided the state needed to get ready.

Major John Morris, a chaplain in the Minnesota Army National Guard who provided a great deal of inspiration in the campaign, described the reintegration process of returning veterans as "going from warrior to citizen." In his frequent speaking appearances, Chaplain Morris has explained that "the army trains individuals for six months to become a warrior. The soldier practices for sixteen months as a warrior. Then three hundred hours from the last mission they return home as a citizen."

One member of the Policy Fellows group, Colonel Eric Ahlness, knew firsthand the challenges facing returning vets and their families from his work as the National Guard liaison to state government, and from his personal experience on deployment to Bosnia and elsewhere. Another group member, Minnesota court of appeals judge Renee Worke, brought her expertise to a number of legal issues returning veterans face. Working with Dennis Donovan, national organizer for Public Achievement at the Center for Democracy and Citizenship (CDC), they adapted community-organizing approaches.

The group found wide support from a bipartisan, bicameral group called the Citizen Legislators, a group of Minnesota state legislators who, with coaching from staff of the CDC, are exploring the role political leaders can play in strengthening civic life. Senator Tarryl Clark from the small city of St. Cloud and Senator Dave Senjem from Rochester, along with Representative Nora Slawik from suburban St. Paul, helped pull the initial group together; Clark and Slawik are Democrats, and Senjem is a Republican.

A key principle of citizen organizing is to build a broad alliance, bringing in people with different strengths, connections, and skills. The Humphrey Institute Policy Fellows, a program of the Center for the Study of Politics and Governance, enlisted a group of public affairs graduate students to be involved in the work on veterans' issues. By the spring of 2007, the CDC had joined the effort as primary organizer. The center recruited individuals and organizations to form a broad coalition including the League of Minnesota Cities, the Citizens League, the Archdiocese of St. Paul and Minneapolis, businesses, both of Minnesota's U.S. senators, and others.

The coalition worked on a number of fronts. It enlisted the help of two talented young communications professionals, Jessie Ostlund and Ellen Tveit, who developed a speaker's bureau to create awareness of challenges and opportunities presented by the return of combat veterans. They also planned a major Warrior to Citizen event at the 2007 Minnesota State Fair. This work soon made it apparent that citizens in many different settings will respond to a campaign built on recognizing the talents and contributions of citizen soldiers returning home. It also became clear that a strong citizen campaign on this question will help to strengthen communities' capacities to work together on other issues.

Returning combat veterans are emphatic in emphasizing that they do not want to be seen as someone who is either broken or a victim. Lieutenant Colonel Tim Kamenar, on leave from the University of Minnesota's Office of Disability Services to work on information engagement with the Minnesota National Guard, spreads the message that veterans have often acquired important skills and experience while deployed. What's more, they have learned and demonstrated a commitment to doing worthwhile civic work, a commitment that needs to be translated into civic life when they return home.

Opportunities for constructive civic work can be vitally important. "Sometimes even the most junior ranking soldier has tremendous responsibilities, much more than fighting. These include building parks; improving physical infrastructure through construction projects, such as building and improving water treatments facilities, wells, and pipelines; helping establish independent local news resources; supporting schools; providing preventive medicine and hygiene training to local communities and schools; and helping establish or reestablish community civil leadership structures and procedures."

Kamenar himself had done a tour of service in Bosnia, and served as a branch chief at the headquarters of the NATO peacekeeping force. "I

TABLE 2

WHAT YOU CAN DO TO HELP THE

WARRIOR TO CITIZEN CAMPAIGN

- If you are a friend or neighbor—and we all are—don't debate the politics of the war, but allow veterans to talk about their experiences. Recognize and show appreciation for their service.

- If you are a member of a faith-based organization, invite a returning veteran to tell his or her story at a service or social event.

- If you work with a youth group, invite a recent veteran to teach young people a new skill.

- If you are a chamber of commerce member, host a job fair featuring opportunities uniquely suited to returning veterans.

- If you are an elected official or sit on a municipal or county board, enlist the expertise of veterans to build your community through board appointments and volunteerism.

was an advisor to a two-star general, and then I went back to anonymity in an office job." This abrupt return and limited ability to readily apply the skills and energy he developed during his service convinced him that many soldiers "want to be engaged in community life, not simply return to private life."

The Warrior to Citizen Campaign matches resources with needs. "Minnesota communities need leadership, experience, competence, and the ability to successfully plan, implement, and execute complex projects," says Kamenar. "If a soldier in a foreign land can work within the constraints of war and multinational politics to create a coalition of citizens, leaders, and soldiers in order to build a water treatment plant, just think of what they can accomplish in their own communities here in Minnesota."

Kamenar also observes the long history of service in the state, intertwined with Minnesota's civic tradition. For instance, the First Minnesota was the Union's first volunteer regiment during the Civil War. Minnesota navy reservists fired the first round of defense during the Pacific campaign of World War II. Minnesota guardsmen of the 34th Infantry became the first American division to ship out for Europe in January 1942. "Going to war and reintegrating are a significant part of what makes Minnesota such an interesting mix of culture and values," Kamenar argues. He notes that while Minnesota's formal politics has tilted in a liberal direction, "the values that pervade most of Minnesota are quite conservative in nature. Service to family, church, community, and working with the military are core elements of how Minnesota has unconsciously identified itself."[7]

Both organizing on global warming and reintegrating veterans as civilian citizens show the ways the new civic movement combines public problem solving with community building. Both activities also begin to create public conversations about issues that have previously not been much talked about. This dynamic of "breaking the silence" is another key ingredient in the civic movement.

Second Civic Skill: Mapping Power and Interests

Everyday civic action in a community, whether a neighborhood, a town, or an institution, involves learning to "think local and act global." This means learning the culture, history, networks, and power dynamics of particular places, whether a school, a neighborhood, or a workplace, and also learning how to act with attention to the larger context. Mapping your environment means looking carefully at the interests and resources around your problem or issue. It helps in developing strategies and taking action.

Remember, your map is important to developing your strategy (described in Chapter 7). Also remember, you'll want to make changes to your map as you take action, learn more about your problem, and build relationships. Remapping is as important as mapping. These maps will change as you talk to new people, get more information, and implement your plans.

TIPS AND TOOLS

Write a few words about your problem or goal in a circle in the middle of a big piece of paper. Then identify who is a part of the environment in which you are working. Where do these people fit in? Where is the team in relation to these other people? As you are creating your map, keep the following two themes in mind:

Map interests: Who is affected by your problem or issue? Your map will identify potential allies your team can work with to address your problem. It will also show people who may create problems or be opposed to your approach. One key early strategy is to try to meet with potential opponents or others who know them, to understand better where they are coming from and whether there might be areas of common ground. As you put people on your map, potential allies or not, make a note of their interests. What is important to them, both in general and specifically related to your problem? Remember, everyday civic politics is about breaking down stereotypes, rigid boundaries, and people's tendency to avoid understanding the views of those that they disagree with.

Analyze power: Who has power over this issue? Who makes the decisions? What kinds of other power do people have, such as position, knowledge, resources like money, moral authority, or relationships? What kinds of power do you have? Think not only about formal power, but informal power as well. What relationships are there, or might there be, between the team and these other people and groups?

3 Breaking the Silence

A group that organized to restore balance in families' hectic lives in some Twin Cities' suburbs also broke the silence on hidden discontents, such as family over-scheduling and the erosion of community life. The group's success has lessons for the surfacing of hidden but widespread cultural discontents. The group raises a question central to the nation's future: how do we educate well-rounded children who are as concerned about the common good as they are about personal success?

TODAY IN MINNESOTA, AS ELSEWHERE, POWERFUL TRENDS threaten civic life. The Minnesota Community Project, created by former vice president Walter Mondale at the Humphrey Institute, noted disturbing trends such as "divisions into increasingly irreconcilable [political] camps . . . deep skepticism about public institutions, and strong disagreements on their role," as well as a sense of declining community as people no longer know their neighbors, suburban fears of increasing immigration, and worry about the state of public schools.[1]

Unease with values touted by the mass culture is often hard for people to talk about. From new immigrants to suburban parents, from inner-city teachers to faculty and students in colleges, people experience "problems that have no name."

At the Center for Democracy and Citizenship (CDC) we first discovered such hidden discontents in 1997, when the Kellogg Foundation asked us to investigate the possibilities for renewing the land-grant public service mission of the University of Minnesota. Edwin Fogelman, chair of the political science department, and I interviewed people who were widely respected in different departments and colleges, seen to embody the ethos or culture of their disciplines and the university, and knowledgeable about its history and operations. Far more than we expected, the interviews uncovered an often painful loss of public purpose. People were alarmed about turf wars, hypercompetitive norms, and the "star system." Faculty members voiced unrealized desires that public engagement be a component of professional work. "Our whole department feels too cloistered," said one department chair, expressing a hope to engage more deeply the urban scene and the public world. Yet across academic disciplines, people said also that they felt increasingly detached even from their departments. "I talk far more to the fifty people in my sub-discipline on the Internet than I do to the people on my hall," said one. And faculty—including many who were extremely successful individually—expressed a deep sense of collective powerlessness to do much about these trends.[2]

There was also pervasive silence. Faculty members said that they avoided mention of their public interests—what had led most of them into academia in the first place—for fear that it might jeopardize their reputations for "rigorous scholarship." They also described the erosion of a sense of departmental community, weakening of the apprenticeship model of relationships with graduate students, and a loss of connection to the local Twin Cities. In subsequent visits to many other campuses in the state and elsewhere, I have found such sentiments to be widespread.

Against this background, we joined with partners to solicit views from Minnesotans about what civic and community values are important to them, what people perceive as threats to community, and what can be done to address the problems and to strengthen our community life. Several thousand Minnesotans participated in house meetings, small group sessions usually held in a home or similar informal setting, and forums in 2006 and 2007.

Many participants mentioned issues regularly discussed in conventional politics—schools, abortion, taxes, race relations, growing income divides, the war in Iraq. But probing for civic values and threats to them also revealed other subjects not so often discussed. People expressed a good deal of anxiety, even fear, that Minnesota's civic culture is endangered. Many voiced the view that a sense of community is eroding. "People in cars don't make eye contact any more in my neighborhood," said one suburban doctor. "I drive into my carport and shut the door, and never talk to my neighbors. It's a culture of me, me, me." Students commonly worried about the erosion of relationships. "We've lost face-to-face human contact. Everyone walks around in their own little iPod world, wired up but tuned out," said Amy Jo Pierce, a student leader at the University of Minnesota. Many feel they live in "bubble cultures," worsened by the way the society pigeonholes people. "When I tell people I'm a Marine and a Christian and a former athlete, they assume I'm a Republican," said Blake Hogan, another student at Minnesota. "But I'm not. People make false assumptions."[3]

Participants in the discussions also identified destructive trends in the mass culture. "Parents in my classes say, in regard to most any topic, 'I've tried fighting society,'" said Sally Wiley, a parent educator with the Minnesota Early Childhood Family Education program. She is a leader in an initiative, Community Based Parent Education, designed to uncover "the public sides of parenting issues." Wiley described typical remarks: "I made my own babyhood, I breastfed, I didn't let my children watch television. For the first two years I fought: fought my family, my friends, ads in the media. I turned off televisions whenever and wherever I could if we were in the room. Now I'm tired, and my kids are being influenced by those things I detest: fast food, 'have it your way,' television programming created as ads to sell products, cross-marketed everything. They are being influenced and I realize I don't have a choice in it."[4]

A number of people expressed concern about excessive consumerism and materialism. "I don't like how children are growing up these days in the consumer culture," said a college student at the Jane Addams School for Democracy who participates in what is called the East African Circle, with East African immigrants. "My family says they can see a big difference between me and my little sister," said a Somali college student in the group. "I grew up in East Africa, and am more oriented to my family and my community. What my little sister cares about is shopping."[5]

In a house meeting with state legislators, Peg Chemberlin, executive director of the Minnesota Council of Churches, said that this dynamic is visible across the state in the religious community. "Increasingly congregants think of themselves as consumers of church, not producers of church, and congregations think of themselves as consumers of denominations, not producers of denominations," Chemberlin said. "In many of our denominations the trend shows up by congregations saying 'We don't like what you're doing, so we're going to quit giving you money,' which is a consumer mentality, understanding themselves as consumers, unobligated to the denomination. We understand that same dynamic to be in play in civic life where we are all too often identified as taxpayers (consumers) rather than citizens (producers)."[6]

Balance 4 Success

It is one thing to identify fears about destructive cultural trends. It is another thing to believe much can be done about them. "Culture change" or "rebuilding community" can sound elusive and abstract. But worrisome trends become concrete and tangible when people organize to address them. A fledgling movement in suburban communities in Minnesota to regain balance in family life and strengthen a sense of community brings the idea of organizing for culture change into focus. These efforts gained media attention in the state and the nation, with coverage in the *New York Times, Newsweek, Family Circle,* NBC and CBS news, and other outlets.

"I went to London a few weeks ago for five days and left my husband a multipage schedule of our sons' activities," *New York Times* reporter Alina Tugend wrote in "Pining for the Kick-Back Weekend." Three weekdays went by with normal school activities. "The weekend was a different story. There were sleepovers, final basketball games, first baseball games, and school plays." Despite their efforts to create some balance — to preserve their own sanity, Tugend and her husband had limited their children to one sport a season, for instance — she realized with a jolt, "how weekends were so jam-packed that Monday came as a relief."

Tugend documented growing complaints among middle-class families and worries among youth development specialists about the dangers of over-scheduling — studies indicate that children have lost nearly one full working day of free time over the last twenty years and high school students rank "not having enough time with parents" as a top concern. She also noted feelings of powerlessness. "It often seems to be something people act as if they have no control over," she said. "A mother I know complains how she misses the days of her childhood when she and her friends just played around their neighborhood on weekends — yet she books her children into every possible activity." But she also observed that "here and there, there are murmurs of protest against filled to the brim weekends."[7] Minnesota leads the way.

Parent-led initiatives have been organized to counteract the over-scheduling of children and the loss of family time in Wayzata, Eden Prairie, and Apple Valley, all suburbs of Minneapolis and St. Paul. Five thousand families in Chaska signed up for family dinners. All are associated with the work of William (Bill) Doherty, a professor of family social science at the University of Minnesota who has come to see himself as a citizen professional, helping families organize to change cultural forces that are overwhelming family life. (His work is described in more detail in Chapter 9.)

The first sign that raising the issue of over-scheduling could tap deep and largely invisible cultural discontents among middle-class families came in Wayzata, when Doherty spoke to a group of parents on the topic. "It was like a revival meeting," Doherty remarked. "Three hundred people showed up." Doherty, working with Barbara Carlson, a parent and civic leader, helped to found the first such group, Putting Family First. Several years later, parents in a crowded middle-school auditorium in Apple Valley, working through a new group, Balance4Success, announced the first boycott of sports on Sundays.

"Parents in middle-class suburbs south of Minneapolis/St. Paul are uniting to liberate their kids from out-of-control sports schedules," read the leaflet inviting people to attend. "Balance4Success, a grassroots organization, wants to change the culture of hypercompetitive childhoods by 'replacing busyness with balance.'"

Other communities addressing issues of out-of-balance schedules and hypercompetitive, overly individualistic suburban cultures had taken mainly educational approaches, stressing the value of family meals together, for instance, or the physical and psychological costs of over-scheduling. Doherty had concluded from the earlier groups' experience that if parents were really to begin to make changes, collective action would be necessary. Strong power dynamics are at work; families often feel intimidated and pressured to fit the norm of hypercompetitiveness. "We're pack animals by nature," as Doherty puts it. "The norm for many in the middle class has become individual competitive success as the highest value, resulting in a culture of hyperactivity. Crazy schedules are now 'bragging rights,'" Doherty told the *New York Times*. "It's not how big your house is and how fancy your car is, but how busy your family is." To counter such pressures, he explained to the *Minneapolis Star Tribune*, "It's time to get edgier." He described Balance4Success's boycott idea as an "edgy" step.[8]

Balance4Success agreed with the idea of collective action, after interviews with families across Apple Valley and other communities in School District 196 convinced them that over-scheduling is a huge but largely hidden issue. The initiative, Taking Back Sundays, was based on their conviction that "the culture of hypercompetitiveness and brutal kids' schedules won't change until parents take concrete, coordinated steps to schedule balance into their kids' lives," as their flyer put it.

In the meeting, the group laid out their thinking and Doherty gave a short talk on the evidence that losing family time together and hyperactivity can be detrimental to children in the long term. As parents responded, I heard again and again anguish that echoed what the early feminist Betty Friedan called "the problem without a name" in the early 1960s. This time the anguish was provoked by the mass culture, not gender roles. I was also struck by the relief people voiced at "breaking the silence." One woman, in tears, said, "I didn't know other people felt this way, too. It's been getting worse and worse." She described friends who put infant children in enrichment activities, touted as necessary for future success and college admissions.

Andrea Grazzini Walstrom, who chaired the meeting, had pulled together a group to work with Doherty the year before. Walstrom, a dynamic woman in her forties, looks like an athlete. In fact she had pioneered breaking the gender line in high school athletics, where she starred in soccer. One interesting feature of the group of parents who organized the boycott is that they were nearly all successful athletes. I asked Walstrom why. "We can see through all the huffing and puffing. We're not intimidated," she replied. She has a deep love of sport. "I know what sports can do, the transformative impact sports can have on kids, their lives, their confidence."

Walstrom, a freelance writer, had written a profile of Doherty for a Minnesota magazine. He discussed the problems he had heard from other parents in other suburbs about over-scheduled kids, pressures of consumerism, and hypercompetitiveness, and the actions they had taken. 'I began to think about my neighbors and family members," she said. "I saw what they struggled with, how they missed family events. Some seemed frantic. Kids' achievements became the driving principle with some families; it became all they were doing."

Walstrom had young children, the oldest being age five. "I began thinking, 'Wow, could this happen to us?'" Hyperactivity violated her sense of healthy development. "What I liked most about preschoolers was quiet time. Kids could spend hours just drawing, or playing with mud. I would come in and out of the room, sometimes talking, sometimes not. I could tell we'd be making meaningful connections. And they weren't fraught with the need to be achieving anything."

She began talking with other families. "Some asked me, 'What have you signed your daughter up for?' They said, 'You shouldn't waste time! If you don't get her in right now it will be too late!' They seemed passionate."

Other parents were more cautionary. "They were not always as intense, but they were thoughtful," Walstrom recalled. "'Be real careful,' they told me. 'This gets carried away real quick. You'll lose your family life. You'll lose your sanity. You'll be driving kids everywhere. Married couples go in opposite directions to separate destinations. Kids are separated. You can't take family trips.' In some of these families there was also the sense, 'What have we gotten ourselves into?'"

She emailed Doherty, who suggested they organize a group to discuss such issues. Walstrom talked to people from the school system, the director of Early Childhood Family Education, a number of parents, a couple of ministers. "They were very supportive of the idea of a grassroots effort. The professionals had more of a sense of it as a big problem than a lot of parents, who experienced it but only within their own families. With educators and public health and public safety people, they saw it every day in their work. Educators would say, 'Kids are coming into school just wiped out.'"[9]

Tim Anderson, a Burnsville pediatrician, underlined the point. Anderson described kids with chronic headaches and stomachaches. "A lot of them suffer from stress and anxiety and they don't know why," he told *Star Tribune* reporter Mary Lynn Smith. "And then we look at their schedules. They have expectations that they have to be on the hockey team, the math team, the debate team. The physical [overuse] injuries they receive from playing too much is tragic. But most of those injuries will heal. The bigger concern is what over-scheduling is doing to their minds and the families."[10]

Parents organized a group named Balance4Success. "We co-opted the idea of 'success,'" explained Walstrom. "Balance is an important ingredient in success, but success needs to be understood in broader, more thoughtful ways." The discussions about what success meant highlighted a number of other dimensions: the ability to have unstructured interactions with others, creativity, self-direction, a sense of morals and connections. It also included learning and instruction from oneself, peers, and parents, not simply other-directed instruction. "All these add to the life of a confident, thoughtful, and responsible — successful — adult," she said. They also discussed the benefits of restorative "down time."[11] "Are we developing a child with a conscience, with a sense of responsibility? Are we creating leaders with thoughtfulness, or are we creating people who are tired, and don't have an individual thought on their own?"

The group also talked about what it means to raise kids who will be civically involved. "If you're not family connected, it makes it very difficult to connect with your community," said Walstrom. "The family is the first neighborhood. You have informal walks, and block parties, and stop along the way. If you're running around from pillar to post, that's not a way to connect with the community. You just become a consumer of what's out there. In a way you're buying your kids' development as a consumer." Some observed that sports create a community, too, but the group decided it was a homogenous group, without essential qualities of civic life like spontaneity and diversity. "The question is what kind of community is the sports community? It's not like your neighborhood or even your church, where all kinds of people are together."

Boycotts raise issues of power and collective action that are far different than conventional middle-class norms. Parents and children have been divided about the boycott idea. "The families that want to play at the more competitive traveling-team level could probably care less about the boycott," said J. D. Grace, who coached his two sons and other children in almost a half dozen sports in Apple Valley. "The only parents who would [sign up for the boycott] would be parents who didn't want their kids to be in sports," said Lucy Mereness, an eleventh grader. Steve and Cheryl Dubbles, whose daughter is on the high school soccer team in Eagan, thought a Sunday free of sports "would be awesome. It's difficult to find time to go to church. Maybe we could even visit Grandma and Grandpa again, instead of having them always come to the soccer field."[12]

Some sports associations — for-profit organized groups with high-powered, often expensive programs for children and teenagers — have fought back. At a public forum on October 4, 2005, directors from several sports associations accused Balance4Success of being "divisive." "It's an individual decision," said one speaker. "Why are you proposing a boycott?"

Walstrom acknowledged their power. She, like others in Balance4-Success, believes that the sports leagues' power to set cultural trends is precisely what requires concerted action. "People down here don't touch the coaches. They're scared to death. The coaches feel like they have power to establish the rules, and they are not afraid to exert that power." The power of the coaches is undergirded by the achievement ethos so central to suburban life. "We seem to have bought the argument that sports is critically important to our kids' development, not just that it's fun or exercise. In Apple Valley we're affluent. There is the issue of scholarships. Success is crucial."

Patterns of informal collusion also exist between high school sports teams and for-profit sports leagues. "In sixth grade, a kid's family in our school district will get a letter from the hockey association, arm in arm with the high school hockey organization, saying that if they want their child to make the varsity hockey team they will need to get on particular teams. Parents listen to that."

The idea of collective action and tension-filled activities like boycotts clearly make some suburban families nervous. "One woman asked me, 'If I get involved, will my child be ostracized?'" said Walstrom. Another had come to the October 4 public forum. She voiced strong opinions about the dangers of over-scheduling, but then backed away, fearful of other parents' reactions. Although many ministers expressed private support, few took a public stand. I asked Grant Stevensen, leader of the Clergy and Religious Leaders Caucus of the ISAIAH group, about this. He had a ready explanation. "It's not the sports directors they're afraid of. It's their own congregations. Ministers have got all these programs that they're running themselves. They're part of the larger patterns. They're often relating to people in their congregations as a service provider. And that's what congregations want, or think they want. Ministers tell me, 'Getting active in social change is not what pays my salary. It's not what my congregation is asking me to do.' Frankly, pastors are going to have to buck the trends. When you go to call committee [the church group that interviews prospective pastors] the members want to know what services you're going to provide, and what services you have experience providing."

For all the obstacles, the unusual effort uncovered dynamics of over-scheduling, consumerism, hyperactivity, and ideas of what parenting should be about. "It broke a silence," Walstrom concluded. "It got people talking. It tapped into a concern that people didn't know how to articulate, or if they did they felt helpless. "Taking Back Sundays is all about the dynamic of being part of something, not all by yourself. That's definitely happened. People are talking about this everywhere, in early childhood classes, in neighborhoods, in coffee houses. People are feeling bolder. It's now a new norm for families to seek balance rather than blindly signing up for anything and everything."[13]

What the boycott accomplishes—how much it changes the behavior of sports leagues, for instance—is connected to other developments. In fact, deep interconnections among issues and settings that seem, on the surface, to have little in common with each other are a powerful factor. Balance4Success raises the question that cuts across every institution: how do we educate young people to be as concerned about community life and the common good as about personal success? At the University of Minnesota, many parallels can also be found. "We're in a fight for the soul of the university," says Gail Dubrow, dean of the graduate school at the University of Minnesota. She described pressures for the university to fit in with the dominant model of high-pressured individualistic scholarship measured in conventional terms like *U.S. News and World Report* rankings, trends that can destroy good teaching, relationships with students, and ties to community. "The question is whether we'll go along with a hypercompetitive culture—or take leadership in the effort to change it."[14]

The question of whether to go along or to take action and develop the power to change a "me first" culture is as relevant in the southern suburbs as it is at the University of Minnesota. Powerful resources from Minnesota's civic history, discussed in the next chapter, can help provide answers.

Third Civic Skill: Holding a House Meeting

A house meeting is a fairly small-group discussion held in a home or some other informal session. It is sometimes among people who know each other, but it is also a good way to get to know friends and acquaintances more deeply through discussion of their interests, values, and ideas for action. House meetings uncover issues or problems and ideas for action that people like you can take. The house meeting shifts the focus of action from what expert might fix the problem, or what government should be doing, to what people like us can actually do to address this question. We have seen this create a large shift in perspective, as simple as it is. House meetings can have many ripple effects.

TIPS AND TOOLS

Focus: It is good to have an issue as the focus of the house meeting. For instance, is there a problem with family over-scheduling in our community?

Recruitment: Participants are invited directly, by personal contact, not by email or leaflet. Six to ten participants are usually best.

Parameters: The meeting will last an hour to an hour and a half. There can be informal socializing after or before.

Style: The meeting should be held in a casual, informal setting like a home or a familiar community site.

Beginning: Begin with a welcome from the host or hostess and offer an explanation of why you think this is an important or useful discussion.

Introductions: Next, present brief statements of the interests that brought people to the meeting; if people don't know each other, there should also be introductions.

Group process: Possible questions:
- What are your experiences with this issue?
  (Stories here are useful, but they should be short.)
- What are values that you and your friends think are important for healthy families and communities?
- Are there things that threaten your values? What are they?

Action: House meetings should include ideas for action.

Next steps: What can people like us do together to take action? Have a concluding discussion on next steps.

4 A History of Adventurous Experiment

The civic heritage of Minnesota, and of each community, is full of lessons to inform and to inspire today's citizen action. The biggest lesson of all is that there is, in fact, a civic heritage. It can help to ground us, give us confidence, and challenge us to the kind of civic greatness that returning veterans call for. It can also provide stories, both good and bad, that we can learn from.

"Perhaps the most attractive feature of the state, after its rare natural beauty, is its refreshing attitude toward adventurous experiment."[1]
WPA FEDERAL WRITERS PROJECT GUIDE TO MINNESOTA, 1938

CIVIC EFFORTS LIKE THE CITIZENS LEAGUE, ORGANIZING to fight global warming at Macalester, the Warrior to Citizen campaign, and Balance4Success build on the state's rich civic heritage. This heritage has combined the efforts of the rich and famous with populist energies. It has also reflected a diverse cultural mix.

Minnesota's history, called by Rhoda Gilman a story of "complicated and conflicting truths," has always involved tensions among diffuse, even contradictory impulses. These differing impulses have been held together by the work of building communities.[2]

A Civic-Minded Establishment

Establishment figures and business elites helped to create a fertile civic context, and perhaps the nation's strongest tradition of corporate citizenship and civic philanthropy. Minnesota's population grew extraordinarily rapidly following its statehood in 1858—from 5,354 in 1850 to 780,773 three decades later, almost three-quarters of whom were first- and second-generation European immigrants. Early economic leaders were exuberant. Speaking of Twin Cities' giants of railroads, lumber, and mining who made their mark, Charles Walker wrote in the classic 1937 book *American City* on the 1934 Minneapolis truckers' strike: "In the decades [after statehood] an unparalleled economic expansion, explosive energy, and an unconquerable optimism had laid the physical foundations" for the mansions that lined Summit Avenue in St. Paul. "That this miraculous expansion would ever cease . . . would have seemed to contemporaries a blasphemy." As a St. Paul newspaper editor put it, "Enclose St. Paul, indeed! Fence in a prairie fire! Bail out Lake Superior! Attempt any other practical thing; but not to set metes and bounds to the progress of St. Paul!"[3]

Business lured immigrants by "high-pressure salesmanship," as the WPA guide put it. Rail and lumber interests often paid them dirt wages and dominated labor camps like a fiefdom. Land grants to the railroads alone in Minnesota—much of it essentially stolen from the Indians—equaled the acreage of two states the size of Massachusetts.[4]

In Minnesota, the rich, however avidly they pursued wealth, often also had a civic side. Many of the state's early European American pioneers came from old Yankee stock in New England, for whom ideas such as the commonwealth, civic responsibility, and educational uplift were crucially important. In the Twin Cities, the "refinements of civilization" were second to none, said observer Julian Ralph. Railroad tycoon James J. Hill's mansion walls were lined with paintings by European masters, while "the literature of two continents, freshened by the constant arrival of the best periodicals, is ready at hand and well marked for use."[5]

The state's leaders created a set of expectations for public and civic contributions. "Second Generation Devoted to Pursuits of Culture," wrote Bertha Heilbron of the Minnesota Historical Society in the special seventy-fifth-year issue of the *St. Paul Pioneer Press* commemorating statehood. "Those who grew up in Minnesota during the period immediately after the Civil War saw Minnesota emerge from a frontier state and grow into a modern commonwealth." She profiled, as an example, Charles M. Loring, president of the Minneapolis park board from 1883 to 1890. Loring laid the foundations for the city's system of parks. "He published articles, gave illustrated lectures, and in various other ways made clear to the people of the state the advantages of parks and civic improvement." Civic efforts spearheaded by leading citizens built libraries and schools, colleges and universities, orchestras, art galleries, theaters and symphonies that complemented the growth of business and industry.[6]

Civic commitments among influential local leaders continued and expanded after World War II. Such leaders created what has been called a "large-system architecture" of civic and public organizations, famous across the country. It included the sanitary district of the 1930s, the airports commission in 1942, the Metropolitan Planning Commission, created by the efforts of Senator Elmer Andersen in 1957, and later the Metropolitan Regional Council. The Urban Coalition emerged out of racial protests and civil rights campaigns in the 1960s, and lasted far longer than in most other cities. Public radio and public television set trends for the nation. The Twin Cities was a center of musical and cultural innovation from the 1930s on, decades before Bob Dylan got his start in the coffee houses around the University of Minnesota and Garrison Keillor began his famous radio career. The cultural scene generated world-famous institutions like the Guthrie Theater, the Minneapolis Institute of Arts, and the Walker Art Center. A rich array of community rooted arts and culture programs have developed alongside and in complicated relationship to these establishment institutions, including Intermedia Arts, Penumbra Theatre, Migizi Communications, and others.

The role of Minnesota philanthropy in sustaining Minnesota civic life is an invisible but crucial part of the establishment's civic history. This tradition of civic philanthropy was built by leaders who served as intermediaries between elites and common people. Russ Ewald, a key architect of the philanthropic tradition, was born in 1921 and grew up on the West Side of St. Paul, a low-income immigrant and working-class community with a vibrant civic culture. Like many there, his house had no indoor bathroom or electricity. "By the time Russ reached third grade, poverty was one thing everyone seemed to have in abundance," wrote Ewald's biographers Jim Storm and Michael Vitt. His alcoholic father abandoned his wife and children as the Depression deepened. His mother, Dorothy, was a dignified, quiet woman who never complained about her poverty but rather stressed education and uplift. "For their entire lives, the Ewald siblings cherished memories of snuggling with their mother as youngsters while she read to them."[7]

After a stint in the Marines during World War II, Ewald became a minister, first with inner city youth in St. Paul, later to the affluent St. Martin's By the Lake parish in Minnetonka, a western suburb in the Twin Cities. Under the surface of wealth, he began to see the turbulent problems that come from hypercompetitive, individualistic, high-pressure lifestyles of the sort that would one day surface in suburbs like Apple Valley. As Storm and Vitt put it, "He repeatedly encountered troubles not expected among the relative affluence of the outer suburbs: alcoholism, abuse, depression, family strife, divorce. And the hard-charging business people of the parish daily ran headlong into serious ethical challenges." Ewald created a pioneering action program that became well known for its innovations in parish ministry, developing initiatives that ranged from social action to civil rights and politics.

Widely respected for a career of public work that had proven responsive to the problems of inner-city young people and affluent suburbanites alike, Ewald was tapped in 1967 by a group of business leaders to develop a new approach to philanthropy. His group, Foundation Services, eventually worked with forty-five foundations to make Minnesota foundations more flexible and responsive. And his most important model, the Minneapolis Equal Opportunity Fund, helped poor and minority people to make down payments on homes and provided startup money for businesses, with the aim of empowering people and communities. This was an approach he later expanded as head of the Minneapolis Foundation and then the McKnight Foundation.

Ewald developed philanthropic approaches that were responsive, respectful, nonbureaucratic, and catalytic. His populist philosophy was expressed in a prominent lecture in 1989. Ewald said, "We are caught up in a time where we are witnessing excesses of arrogance throughout the society: a stockbroker who manages to make $500 million in one year; athletes who receive several million in salaries; corporate executives who receive million-dollar bonuses while thousands of employees at the same company are being laid off. . . . Philanthropy is being judged as to whether it is liberating the lives of those individuals who are trapped in the morass of poverty."

Ewald ruffled many feathers as he challenged dominant values. He also served as a bridging figure between the establishment and movements of the people. Minnesota's civic life has been mostly created by common people, unsung heroes and heroines. People raise children, care for the elderly, earn a living, and work to build healthy communities. Sometimes their efforts have combined in broad populist movements that have revived the wider democracy itself.

Minnesota's Populist Legacy

"Today is election day," the American philosopher John Dewey wrote from Ann Arbor, Michigan, to his wife, Alice, in 1894. "I should like to have voted for a few Populists." There were only a few members of the Populist Party in Michigan. But there were a lot in Minnesota, where he had just spent a year at the University of Minnesota. Throughout his life, Dewey referred positively to the Populist Party, formed in 1892. Leaders of the Populist Party, in his view, were "fundamentally sound in their opposition to the growing power of wealth."[8]

The populist movement included the Populist political party, also known as the People's Party, formed in 1892 by the merger of farmers' cooperatives, the Knights of Labor, and other groups. Minnesotans played leading roles in its formation. The flamboyant Minnesota politician, editor, and stump speaker Ignatius Donnelly wrote most of the platform. Minnesota continued to send populist politicians to the U.S. Congress after the People's Party's demise. Following Floyd Olson's election as governor in 1930, populist policies shaped mainstream state politics. Hubert Humphrey, a key architect of the merger of the Farmer-Labor Party and the Democratic Party in 1944, voiced his own identification with the populist tradition. Humphrey described his faction of the Democratic-Farmer-Labor Party (DFL) as "Populist liberals, Farmer-Laborites . . . and ardent New Dealers."[9]

Populism in Minnesota, as elsewhere, was a much broader and older movement than its constituent political parties. Its slogan, "the people in politics," had deep historical roots. It also drew from eighteenth- and nineteenth-century traditions such as Jeffersonian democracy in the United States and Scandinavian folk schools, which also had a strong influence in the midwestern state of Minnesota. Populism took political shape in both Russia and the United States in late-nineteenth-century agrarian movements blending traditions of mutual aid, independence, small property, and civic uplift.[10]

Populism grew from a grassroots tradition that both complemented and challenged elites from the beginning of statehood. Understood as grassroots practices that build the civic agency of ordinary people, populism also has roots in earlier Native American traditions.[11] Though less visible, the populist values and efforts of those Charles Walker called "the rank and file"—farmers, mineworkers, factory workers, artisans, truck drivers, teachers, and others—has been the deep wellspring of Minnesota civic life.

In the spirit of adventurous experiment, an egalitarian and democratic culture spurred immigrant growth. Swedish immigrants wrote thousands of "America letters." One described "the democracy that obtained in the new country. . . . Caste lines in Sweden were severely restrictive [but] here was a land where everyone was a landlord and servants sat down to table with the masters." "I am my own master, like the other creatures of God," wrote another immigrant, after two and a half years in Minnesota. "Neither is my cap worn out from lifting it in the presence of gentlemen. There is no class distinction here between high and low, rich and poor, no make-believe, no 'title sickness' or artificial ceremonies."[12]

Civic learning and uplift, as well as practical organizing around gritty issues like freight rates and grain prices, infused grassroots movements for reform in the state from the beginning. In 1866 Olson H. Kellogg founded the National Grange of the Order of the Patrons of Husbandry, a secret society among farmers that organized cooperatives and fought to control economic concentrations of power, establishing the principle that railroads and other corporations "clothed with public interest" were properly subject to public regulation. The Grange, open to women as well as men, emphasized social and intellectual enrichment of rural life, sponsoring a variety of educational efforts.

The Farmer's Alliance, a network of cooperatives that built on the Grange in the 1880s across the state, organized neighborhood gatherings, newspapers, lectures, and reading circles, as well as cooperatives. Suffragists in Minnesota drew on their efforts, combining the fight for equal rights with reading circles and book clubs. Suffragists often led in the creation of libraries.

A striking example of this civic learning culture came with the Farmer-Labor Association of the 1920s, 1930s, and early 1940s. The Association — legally separate from the Farmer-Labor Party that for a time controlled the governorship and the state legislature — focused on self-help and education. Its philosophy was expressed by the *Minnesota Leader*, the leading populist paper in the state, with a circulation of 150,000 by 1936. The *Leader*, according to the state's leading populist historian, Thomas O'Connell, "was both the house organ of the Association and a mirror of the diverse and pluralistic nature of the movement as a whole." It included stories of cooperatives, news of labor battles across the state and nation, and developments in Washington. It also included a good deal of coverage of Scandinavian social movements. "The *Leader* spoke in many tongues," O'Connell wrote, "to dirt farmers, professionals, small-town businessmen, and urban workers. It spoke to old prairie populists and young professionals."[13]

The *Leader* was a major source of discussion in the Farmer-Labor Association clubs that sprang up across the state. Clubs were organized on either a township or ward level. When ten or more people expressed interest, a new club could be chartered by the state headquarters in St. Paul. Many trade unions and some farm organizations formed the basis of the Farmer-Labor Association in the 1920s. In the 1930s, thousands of citizens, farmers, workers, and many members of the middle class signed up and created clubs. A major push to form Farmer-Labor clubs began in 1932, the second year of Olson's administration. The Association put organizers on the road to set up clubs, supplying pamphlets, books, information on issues, ideas for club agendas and, especially, speakers for local clubs. Leaders and educators crisscrossed the state, organizing lectures and discussions, helping to spark civic life in communities.

Club meetings typically included a social hour, a recitation, often with a religious theme, and a community sing. Club meeting agendas varied widely, with open forums, wide-ranging discussions of local issues, readings from newspapers, and other events. By 1935 each club was to have an educational secretary who helped design programs. Many encouraged "study circles," ongoing educational and discussion groups that drew from Scandinavian folk school traditions of popular education. Some organized libraries—Montevideo, Red Wing, Sandstone, and Whitfield gained special attention.

Populist educators were aware that lectures and discussions were not sufficient. A manual of the Farmer-Labor Educational Bureau (established in 1934 to systematize and to expand educational efforts) stressed music and social interactions. "Music will ease the tension . . . any local artist, accordion, piano, violin, banjo, harmonica, are fine." It encouraged clubs to organize picnics, dances, amateur shows, and similar events. In many areas Farmer-Labor Association clubs became centers of social life. They also were activist. For instance, Farmer-Labor Association chapters often organized cooperatives.

By the late 1930s, the Farmer-Labor Association included tens of thousands of members. Union membership remained more or less steady through the decade—between 6,000 and 10,000 members. But individual membership, less than 1,000 in 1930, had climbed to 14,000 by 1934 and 20,000 in official numbers by 1937. O'Connell estimated that at least as many more were involved unofficially. In the mid-1930s there were 3,500 Association members in the Twin Cities and another 1,600 in Duluth.[14]

In recent years the populist legacy has reemerged on both sides of the partisan divide. Republicans such as former governor Al Quie have continued the populist tradition through their emphasis on active civic involvement. As a Republican congressman in the 1960s, Quie was an outspoken champion of civil rights. In a little-known show of support, he offered office space to the group camped out in Resurrection City in 1968, part of Martin Luther King's populist Poor People's Campaign.

Governor Quie has also brought a populist perspective to subsequent citizen efforts. For instance, he has been a strong and effective voice for a family and community-based approach to early childhood education to counter the dangers of a professional takeover of early childhood, and a champion of a campaign to integrate former prisoners back into the life of communities as contributing citizens.

On the other side of the aisle, the populist tradition was powerfully continued by the late Paul Wellstone and the civic organization that bears the name of he and his wife, Sheila, Wellstone Action. Democratic political leaders such as former vice president Walter Mondale, Minnesota secretary of state Mark Ritchie, and representative Kate Knuth, have also powerfully voiced populist themes.

The underlying impulse of populism is a deep respect for the agency of ordinary people and strategies and approaches to develop people's talents and central role in democracy. Today "the people" is more diverse a concept than was often earlier understood.

Minnesota as a Cultural Crossroads

Despite conventional wisdom about "the white bread" state, Minnesota has always been a state of cultural diversity. Sometimes this had positive outcomes. In the eighteenth century, the fur trade and intercultural exchanges and marriages among Indians and Europeans produced "mutual accommodation" of Indian and European styles, technologies, and attitudes.[15]

John Radzilowski portrayed a scene at Grand Portage during trading season: "Grand Portage bustled with activity, color, and life. There one could hear Ojibwe and other Algonquin dialects, French in varying forms, and increasingly after 1763, English spoken with British, Scottish, and American accents. Native quill work and bright European fabrics contrasted with drab woolen wear and buckskin or the dark robes of Jesuit priests. . . . Wintering voyageurs arrived to trade for fresh supplies, to drink, dance, and party. Marriages with local Native

American and mixed race women 'by the custom of the country' were common."[16]

Sometimes marriages were transient. But many produced not only deep, sustained relationships but also worked to create a distinctive cultural group, the Métis. By 1800, at least 30,000 Métis lived in Minnesota, southern Canada, and lands further west. "The Métis prided themselves on having the best of both worlds," writes Nicholas Vrooman. "Their European-style clothing was adorned in Indian fashion, often blending beadwork and tartans, symbols of their tribal and clan heritage. For entertainment they played the fiddle but employed a drum rhythm, and they danced the jig in an Indian manner. Deeply religious, they prayed to Jesus, yet sang medicine songs of healing. . . . From their two heritages, they created a new language, Michif, a beautiful blending of French nouns and Indian verbs."[17] The Métis were not a homogenized melting pot but rather a creative synthesis, the integration of cultural and racial differences into something that had powerful roots and that was also rich and innovative.

By the threshold of statehood in 1858, respect for Indians had been replaced among most whites by hostility and hunger for their land. In 1851 leaders of the Dakota, facing military threats, gave up almost all of their land west of the Mississippi, with the exception of a reservation in the Red River Valley. In 1862, a group of young Dakota warriors, starving and humiliated, attacked settlers on the western border of the state. The U.S. military response was savage. The population of the Red River reservation was forcibly removed, even though most had opposed the attacks. In the largest mass execution in U.S. history, thirty-eight Indians were hanged on December 26, convicted with little evidence. Among the dead was Chief Chaska, who had vigorously opposed the attacks and had saved the life of a settler, Sarah Wakefield.

Contradictory elements like this, acts of synthesis, creativity, and generosity contrasting with raw prejudice, savage inequalities, and bitter conflicts, have threaded throughout the state's history. On the more admirable side, during the same years that Minnesota scandalously betrayed its promises to Indians, the First Minnesota, a regiment of farmers and shopkeepers, Germans, Swedes, Irish, and Yankees, were among the first to volunteer for the Union army. They achieved legendary status for their acts of heroism. At the battle of Gettysburg, a year after the great massacre of Indians, the 262 surviving members of First Minnesota, outnumbered more than eight to one by Confederate soldiers, charged the Alabama regiments and turned back the attack on the key position at Cemetery Ridge, the center of the Union line of defense. Many believe their actions saved the day, and perhaps the Union itself.

The members of First Minnesota helped to establish a long tradition of leadership in the fight for racial justice and inclusion that has characterized Minnesota's civic life ever since. Hubert Humphrey's famous speech at the 1948 Democratic convention demanding a fair employment plank was an example. So was Al Quie's offer as a Republican congressman in 1968 of office space to those encamped in Resurrection City. In 2006 Keith Ellison was elected to congress from the Fifth Congressional District, the first Muslim to hold national office.

But the picture is complicated. While Minnesotans have sometime taken leadership in civil rights, African Americans and other cultural and racial minorities have suffered from raw discrimination and violence. A mob in Duluth, inflamed by rumors of rape, lynched three young African American men in 1920. In the 1930s, Minneapolis was known as the nation's capitol of anti-Semitism. In many communities, stigmatized cultures have included German and Scottish, Italian, Irish, and Finnish, Catholics, Jews, even Swedes and Norwegians.

Such ironies can be traced to differing conceptions of American identity. At its inclusive best, Minnesota's civic life has affirmed a view of the American people as organized most importantly by democratic ideals, the values of the Declaration of Independence, and the preamble to the Constitution: all are created equal; all have a right to liberty and justice; the people, not any elite, establish government to promote the general welfare. Yet this version of Americanism has also conflicted with narrower and more fearful ideas of who an American is, based on race or culture or religion, economic status or celebrity, claiming that "real Americans" exclude new immigrants, or racial minorities, or those of different religious beliefs.

These conflicts continue today, as national controversies over immigration have surfaced again in the state as well. In recent years, the state has seen a major increase in immigration from Latin America, Southeast Asia, and East Africa. And on March 8, 2006, forty thousand marchers in St. Paul called for reform in the nation's immigration laws. "Driven by our vision of a shared future where all of us are full participants, ISAIAH leaders and our allies are . . . working to educate and build relationships with our neighbors and legislators, standing up to demand just, humane policies toward the immigrants in our communities," declared the newsletter of the bipartisan church-based citizen organization called ISAIAH, in its April 2006 issue. But much of the state—like the nation—reacted in fearful ways. Bills were introduced in the Minnesota legislature to force local authorities to collect and report immigration status information, make county health workers report undocumented immigrants to federal officials, outlaw ordinances in Minneapolis and St. Paul sympathetic to immigrants, and create a body to enforce federal laws—the first such statewide law enforcement team.[18] Across the state immigrants experienced discrimination, fear, and hostility.

Free Spaces — Meeting Grounds in Community Life

If democratic, inclusive values are to survive and flourish in our communities, there must be plentiful living environments where they can be woven into everyday life. These can be called free spaces, civic meeting grounds for diverse people, wellsprings of civic life. Phyllis Wheatley Settlement House on the north side of Minneapolis was an example. Phyllis Wheatley house was part of the Twin Cities Federation of Settlements (TCFS), a group of eleven settlement houses in the 1920s and 1930s. The federation's mission was "to develop neighborhood forces, arouse neighborhood consciousness, to improve standards of living, incubate principles of sound morality, promote a spirit of civic righteousness, and to cooperate with other agencies in bettering living, working, and leisure-time conditions."[19]

Settlement houses typically had staff living on site "in order to ensure that those employed understood the local community dynamics and undertook all their work from that vantage." They stressed working *with* neighborhood residents and new immigrants, rather than "ministering unto" them. According to the federation, this meant that settlements did most of their work through "the influence and power of example."

Many settlements aimed at educating college students to think of themselves as citizens, working with residents and immigrants who were fellow citizens of the neighborhood. Sometimes students from the University of Minnesota lived in upstairs rooms. Gertrude Brown, the director, was a visionary civil rights leader who each year would give a speech about the progress of the freedom movement.

Lori Sturdevant, in her biography of Harry Davis, a school board member who was also the first black elected official in Minnesota, describes how the Wheatley house became the civic meeting ground for the broad African American community in North Minneapolis. "It is fair to say that Phyllis Wheatley Settlement House is what brought the African Americans of North Minneapolis together into a functioning community," Sturdevant writes. "The Wheatley settlement provided [blacks] with self-awareness and pride. It fostered relationships. It taught people to help one another and to raise their families in a difficult and challenging environment."[20]

The formative experiences of Richard Green, a leading American educator who grew up in the 1940s and 1950s, illustrated her observations. His experiences revolved around black churches, extended family networks, and especially, he said, the Phyllis Wheatley Settlement House, the heart of the African American community. Green remembered Wheatley as a community commons, a civic center full of public activities and extended relationships that shaped his vision for what public schools should be: a commons for the modern age. His vision, in turn, inspired educators and families in Minneapolis, where he served as school superintendent in the 1980s, and led him to be chosen chancellor of New York public schools, before an untimely death. Like the commons of old, Green told *Minneapolis Star Tribune* reporter Kay Miller, Wheatley was "the focal point" of social life and more. It taught values of hard work, self-discipline, accountability, achievement, and giving back. "Even though we were not a community of wealth, it certainly was a community of cooperation and helping the young people grow up in a healthy manner." Settlement workers and others who sustained Wheatley "would smack your ass in a minute if you got out of line."[21]

Over the years, settlement houses have tended to become social service centers—an identity that none would have recognized fifty years ago. But nothing is static, neither civic renewal nor civic decline. Today, other civic meeting grounds in diverse neighborhoods have also appeared, a new generation of free spaces that reconnect education to the life of communities while developing people's sense of confidence, culture, and power. The Cultural Wellness Center, in the ethnically diverse Phillips and Powderhorn neighborhoods of Minneapolis, is a striking example.

Fourth Civic Skill: Finding Free Spaces in Your Community
Free or public spaces are places of, for, and by the public. Look for "Humphrey drugstores," civic meeting grounds like the store that educated Hubert Humphrey (see Chapter 1). They are important because the natural tendency is to stick with people who are like us. People who are different can make us uncomfortable, but they are necessary for building civic muscle.

Free spaces are places to socialize, discuss, have fun, learn and do public work. There are free public spaces in every community. They are settings where people meet as equals with others who are outside their immediate family and friendship circles, where people have a sense of comfort and ownership, and where people learn values and habits of public life, such as regard for the common good. Look for places where people who may disagree on topics like partisan politics interact and get to know each other.

TIPS AND TOOLS

Map free spaces: You get a feel for free spaces by trying to identify them in the community. Public spaces might include community centers, locally owned businesses (coffee houses, corner stores, etc.), libraries, park and recreation centers, schools with a strong neighborhood connection, front porches, or churches used by the community.

Going public: One way for communities to claim free spaces is to make them visible. A way to do this is to make a public display. Using photos, storyboards, art, and other means, make a display or exhibit that highlights free spaces in your community and what happens there.

Growing free spaces: Another key aspect of free-space building is to strategize with others about how to create them. You might hold a community conversation or house meetings on strengthening free spaces. What free spaces now exist? How can you help create new ones?

5 Cultural Leaders

A community-based cultural organization rooted in the African American experience offers a key lesson for today's citizen movement. When the goal is change toward a more community-oriented, egalitarian society, we can look to groups that have been seen by some as oppressed or marginalized for leadership on the pressing questions of our time, such as how we educate our children to be socially connected and concerned citizens, as well as be successful in their personal and work lives.

I N TODAY'S DOMINANT CULTURE, STRONG ATTACHMENT TO community values can actually doom kids to failure. Low-income and working-class children are often likely to do poorly in school and later careers, feel powerless in relation to institutions, and get little encouragement for educational and civic uplift of the sort that once animated places like the Phyllis Wheatley Settlement House. These settlements grounded learning in a myriad of experiences that involved extended families, friends, and many diverse figures in the neighborhood. And as the former Minneapolis school superintendent Richard Green observed, the values and principles of such informal community learning sites often informed public schools more than the other way around. The consequence of the loss of the tie between education and community settings is a terrible trade-off between community and individual achievement today that harms middle-class suburbanites as surely as it harms poor people, if in a different way.[1]

To reintegrate community and education will mean recalling traditions like Phyllis Wheatley and the other settlement houses that showed that human learning involves far more than individual achievement. The Powderhorn Phillips Cultural Wellness Center in Minneapolis conveys similar lessons. It draws on the richness of learning and cultural resources in African American and other indigenous cultural experiences and traditions. It has an intellectual, experiential, and futurist frame that "evens the playing field," in the words of co-founder Atum Azzahir, a place for mingling and interaction among diverse peoples by respecting people's heritages.[2] It also shows that knowledge-production about community life and health often occurs far from academic settings.

The Cultural Wellness Center also raises questions that leaders believe were missing from the explicit goals of the civil rights movement. The movement—with some important exceptions—was framed by the demand for equal rights to be integrated into the dominant culture. But what if the dominant culture was moving toward a version of the American dream that neglected community and the common good?

A Site of Wisdom and Hope

"A lot of people these days are working hard to try to recreate democracy. Everybody is sick and tired of the segregation and the selfishness. But we don't have examples of the cultural peoples having the space where their wisdom is used as part of what is created. That's what we bring. I think we have a lot to teach," says Azzahir, cofounder with her colleague Janice Barbee of the Cultural Wellness Center.[3]

Azzahir is a great public intellectual who never went to a traditional college. She reminds me of other public intellectuals I knew in the black freedom movement. Though Azzahir did not get a conventional degree from college, she is widely read and studies systematically at her husband's institute of African philosophy, the International Khepran Institute. She also reflects constantly, with others at the Cultural Wellness Center, on the theory, lessons, and models they are developing. With her colleague Barbee, Azzahir also teaches undergraduate and graduate students from different fields at the Academic Health Center and other departments of the University of Minnesota.

The purpose of the Cultural Wellness Center is "to unleash the power of citizens to heal themselves and to build community." The center's philosophy is based on the proposition that "health results from the process of people's active engagement and participation in life, in defining the standards of health for themselves, and in addressing sickness and disease on the community and cultural as well as personal levels." It grew out of a two-year process of listening and engaging people in conversation across the area. This philosophy also has powerful implications for educating young people.[4]

The Cultural Wellness Center is located in a bank building on the border of the South Minneapolis Powderhorn and Phillips neighborhoods. This is the most culturally diverse area in Minnesota, with the largest combined concentration of African Americans, Native Americans, Asians, and Latinos. The neighborhoods also include many people from diverse European American traditions.

The interior of the center reflects the cultures, images, and traditions of the community. Plants along the walls seem to flourish in the space. Masks from East and West Africa hang alongside textiles from Southeast Asia and Celtic images. When one enters, the sounds of water fountains and the smell of cedar, sage, or frankincense and myrrh generate the sensation of being in a different kind of place, rooted, alive.

Azzahir's prior experiences included a stint as director of the Harriet Tubman Center, one of the nation's pioneering battered women's shelters, and as director of Way to Grow, a highly successful early childhood educational initiative that was Minneapolis mayor Don Fraser's signature initiative in the 1980s. Azzahir combines such experiences with a remarkable presence — somehow she embodies the philosophy and spirit of the center. She seems wise, grounded, infused with a sense of plural voices that made me think of Walt Whitman's poetry.[5]

In the mid-1990s, Azzahir teamed up with Mike Christianson, director of the giant Medica Health Plans, which she had recruited as a partner to Way to Grow. They explored the idea of focusing on one place, South Minneapolis, through the prism of her core philosophy, and Medica provided financial resources. "Rather than focusing on what was wrong with Black people — that they have high infant mortality rates, and other public health problems — I wanted to explore the other side: Why it is that some children live and flourish in the exact same conditions?" she says. "What are the sources of resilience? What is it that gave us as African American people the capacity sometimes to transcend the conditions that were terribly oppressive?"[6]

The three principles behind their philosophy, what they call the People's Theory of Sickness, include the idea that people are responsible for their own recovery and healing; that community provides the container and the resources for living a healthy life; and that connection to culture and a sound identity transform the historical trauma of racism.

Azzahir and Barbee — who came to her own passionate commitment to cultural restoration seeing her own family, of Welsh descent, buffeted and torn apart by the medical system because of her brother's schizophrenia — spent two years holding conversations with different cultural communities in South Minneapolis. They discovered that other cultural groups — Hmong, Latinos, Native Americans, and European Americans as well — had similar issues. "I know of the collective aloneness of the African American because I am a member of this group," said Azzahir, "but to hear the Dakota, Lakota, Nakota, and Ojibwe people, Mexican and Hmong American people speak of their deep sense of disconnectedness and aloneness has amazed me. I thought these groups had culture, language, and a home base, even if they didn't control it. I became more and more driven to be a part of and give direction to an effort to alleviate this condition for these great peoples of ancient heritage." She credits her partner, Barbee, for understanding that what they call "cultural restoration" is urgent and meaningful for people of European descent as well as other "great peoples of ancient heritage."[7]

Azzahir and Barbee gathered hundreds of people in Citizen Health Action Teams, or CHATS, that took place biweekly and monthly. The meetings were a place for discussion of sickness, disease, health and medical practices, crime, violence, race, class, religion and spirituality, family education, jobs, old age, sexuality, and other topics. "Of these, sickness and disease levels and health and medicine drew the broadest response, and also affirmed the emphasis we had placed on these topics before we began organizing," Azzahir and Barbee wrote. The process also clarified their theory of knowledge generation. "This highly active process of bringing together many different people from many different cultures to solicit solutions to a community's problems became our trademark. It is now the approach we use in the center for sustaining people's engagement, as well as generating organic knowledge that helps solve the problems facing community residents."[8]

Azzahir and Barbee and others connected to the center organize their work into three areas. The first, the Invisible College, explicitly addresses the meaning of education for people of all ages. It involves an extensive series of class offerings, including cultural competence courses for professionals. Of relevance to communities everywhere, it also consciously challenges the overly professionalized views of education that dominate today.

Thus, a class on old ways of parenting begins with parents asking what kind of values and practices they want to teach their children, how they want them to grow up, and what their traditions have to say about preparing children to contribute to community life. This, in Azzahir's account, helps families — many of whom feel marginalized or discounted by public school educators today — reclaim their heritage as a source of wisdom and power. Other elements of the Invisible College similarly emphasize cultural resources. The class on keys to self-care involves intergenerational learning about the wisdom that comes from different communities' experiences with survival, struggle, and endurance. Others features of the class include developing one's family tree, eating foods of one's ancestors, exploring different cultural ways of understanding the end of life, and heritage as a key to self-care.

The faculty composition makes a powerful statement in itself. Teachers are elders and others knowledgeable about cultures' ways of knowing. They are chosen and prepared through reflection and immersion within cultural traditions.

The second area of work is called Core Member Services. These include a variety of cultural health practices drawn from different traditions, including yoga, martial arts, movement, and dance, with many members of the community contributing skills and knowledge. This area has generated a variety of organizing initiatives, including the African American Men's Support Network, the Coalition of African Women Rebuilding Our Communities, Lakota, Dakota, and Nakota Grandmothers' Society, and European American Mothers' Circle.

The third area, the Health Program, is guided by a woman who spent twenty years practicing conventional medicine. In 1996, she began a learning transition that returned her to the Haitian heritage, which she had once felt pressured to leave behind and forget. "She is now guiding the Center's teaching of other health and social service professionals along with the Cultural Elders," write Azzahir and Barbee. The self-health assessment tool developed by the center shows a person's progress from isolation and detachment from cultural roots to health and wellness, a sense of belonging, strong cultural identity, and participation in vital community life.

Powerful threads weave through Azzahir's life and work, from her childhood in the little Mississippi delta town of Grenada to the Cultural Wellness Center today. These show deep resources in the African

American experience for addressing the cultural discontents of modern America. I explored these in an interview after the first meeting of the state working group of Minnesota Works Together, a coalition formed on April 13, 2006, to strengthen civic life in the state. We held the meeting in the Invisible College room at the center, which seemed symbolic.

At the meeting, Azzahir remarked that the Cultural Wellness Center's core philosophy, cultural wellness and restoration, represented a change in her approach. "I had worked from a frame of oppression theory for the previous thirty years. I'd done anti-racism work in every form. I gave up anti-racism training because it does not deal with the spirit, and the spiritual debasement that has happened on both sides."[9]

I wanted to know more about what she meant. From observing hundreds of citizen groups over the last thirty years and interviewing hundreds of civic leaders in groups fighting for voice and power, I had come to believe that typical questions in citizen activism — How are we oppressed? Who is the enemy? How can we defeat them? — can all too easily reinforce a culture of victimhood, powerlessness, and dependency. And they neglect the lessons I had learned as a young man from leaders like Martin Luther King and Dorothy Cotton—it is usually more effective in changing patterns of prejudice and bigotry to find democratic aspirations in a culture than to attack from the outside.

The oppression theory that Azzahir had named also assumes that the highly individualized, hypercompetitive, and over-scheduled lives of the upper middle class are the norm toward which everyone else should aspire. But I knew enough about the discontents surfacing in Apple Valley and other suburbs — and about the erosion of the civic mission of schools — to know that we could use insights from leaders who were thinking about what communities and cultural groups could offer to education and to the wider society.

Azzahir explained her remarks on oppression especially in terms of its inadequate theory of power, which stresses "power over" not "power to." Her work in the battered women's movement had taught her that "fighting your way out of oppression just doesn't work, and hasn't worked for a long time. You have to wrangle power from people." She had also seen that African American women, in particular, when they thought of themselves simply as victims, often "didn't go anywhere. They started to use the shelter as a respite, and then they would go back and do the same thing."

So she changed. "I began to live the idea that you have to build relationships, and become part of networks, and watch how important it is for everyone to have an agenda that is in their own interests — not simply individual interests but collective interests. I have built my life work around that idea since then. It's about restoration of culture, too."

Culture is the central theme for the Cultural Wellness Center, the foundation for individual health and also for raising healthy children as communities and a society. The first time we discussed the idea of an effort across the state to strengthen civic life, in the winter of 2006, Azzahir told me the story of a recent experience she had had, talking to a group of teenagers about potential medical careers. One Hmong student said he struggled with the idea, because he felt he would have to give up his culture if he entered a medical profession. Azzahir asked the others what they thought. There was silence from the group, all European Americans. Then one remarked, "I don't have a culture. I live in the suburbs. My culture is shopping and playing video games." "I really got mad," Azzahir told me. "I told them that was crazy; they needed to learn who they are."[10]

Azzahir's strong sense of cultural heritage came from her childhood, when she developed a strong sense of identity that was grounded in a Southern black community where her family owned a small piece of land. "It was in a hotbed of hatred, segregation, and uprootedness that I learned how to create a space where well-being can happen even under the most devastating circumstances," she said. "This lesson was taught religiously by my mother, who cared for my father during his frail times. She worked as a maid and a babysitter from sunup to sundown. She retained her grace and beauty because her sisters, mother, and daughters provided an ever-replenishing source of support. Her long view of life refreshed her spirit when the demands of maintaining the life support of other people weighed on her."

The larger black community helped as well. "We resolved personal conflict and family disturbances by going to church, dancing, story-telling, and singing. We saw a relationship between a strong community and personal strength, harmony, and survival skills. Many of the old people talked in codes to each other, averted the dangers, and stood constantly in vigilance and prayer. The children were granted child-hood, and allowed to escape the burdens of life, at least through adoles-cence. It was the tradition to teach, transfer skills, and assure that each generation survived."

Azzahir said, "I saw my parents treated horribly, and they still could laugh. Their dignity was amazing. They taught us, 'Think for yourself. Take care of yourself! Do the things you need to do to protect yourself.' The experience of segregation was much more brutal for people who had to go out and ask for help. So we needed to build jobs and institu-tions to be self-reliant." Mutual aid and self-reliance were core traits of the African American experience. I knew from previous research in Baltimore that these values were often carried over into schools and other community institutions. In Baltimore the black school tradition dated to well-known institutions such as Sharp Street, established in the eighteenth century; African School, founded in 1812 by Daniel Coker; and girls schools such as St. Francis Academy. In the decades of segre-gation, schools like Frederick Douglass High School and Morgan State were seen as beacons of black education, turning out national leaders like Lillian Jackson of the NAACP, Clarence Mitchell, the famous lawyer, and Congressman Parren Mitchell. The schools, in turn, were grounded in dense networks of community life and other institutions in the black community.[11]

Azzahir understood well the multidimensional power and richness of the African American educational and civic tradition. "I learned that the spirit of resiliency was rooted in my blackness. This blackness, which was hated and cursed by outsiders, was cultural, spiritual, political, educational, and social. I was taught the honor in blackness, that blackness was the social capital for the business of living instead of a reason for dying."

The pattern that Azzahir began to see when she moved to Milwaukee at the age of nineteen was that as powerful as the freedom movement for dignity and equality was, it also made the mistake of taking for granted the depth and resiliency of the black community and its institutional and social life. Thus the goal of inclusion in mainstream American society, especially the public schools, neglected to ask what was being given up, or how the mainstream might have to be transformed. "With a more open society, we slowly began to pursue outside jobs and schooling and learn outside values. The movement for human dignity became a movement for equal rights. We were swept along with the wave of integration within schools and other public facilities." The tragedy, in Azzahir's view, is that "the black psychological, social, cultural, and emotional infrastructure that had endured through the unprecedented brutality of slavery and Jim Crow was now not valued but devalued and redefined." Azzahir saw a considerable irony. Children were bussed to school. Many sang, "We're free at last." But what did freedom entail?[12]

In her view, the reason for African American children's problems in public schools has largely to do with the clash between the communal values of the black cultural tradition and the individualist, culturally detached quality of these schools — just the values and dynamics that Balance4Success is seeking to counter in a different environment, European American suburbia. Her observations also complement the findings of scholars such as David Mathews and Annette Lareau, described in Chapter 8, that the civic and cultural dimensions of education have become eclipsed in recent decades. Azzahir describes her intention at the center as "trying to create for others the good experience I had growing up." The values and practices of community, of cultural heritage, of resilient families, of elders' wisdom are all essential, in her view, to health. They are also central to raising children to be socially connected and concerned, as well as individually successful.

Since these are the values that Minnesotans — and Americans more generally of diverse cultural backgrounds and income levels — feel are endangered in a me-first culture, the work of the Cultural Wellness Center has a prophetic quality and also a leadership role. It can help others to see beyond present patterns to future possibilities that tie community life to education. The next chapter will look at ISAIAH, a citizen group in Minnesota that has also taken up the questions of culture and learning, in a different way.

Fifth Civic Skill: Discovering Cultural Resources

Cultural resources contribute to a community's civic capacities. Every community has cultural resources — including those communities that seem homogenous, or "without culture." Culture is "the way we do things around here" — traditions, norms, values, practices, rituals, symbols, and other things that express and sustain relationships. A neighborhood typically has a number of cultures, and also an overall culture tied to the place. There are often many conflicts among them. Learning to see cultural dimensions is a crucial skill for effective civic action and dealing with differences.

TIPS AND TOOLS

Identify your needs: Who might have a good eye for cultures in the community? What do you need to know?

Do one-on-one interviews: Here the point is less to find out about people's individual self-interests than the cultural life of a place.

Look for stories: Don't approach an interview with the idea of solving any particular problem. Think oral history—who can tell about what is valued in this neighborhood or group? What are the hidden mores? Who are the heroes? What are the symbols?

Evaluate: After the meeting, ask yourself what went well, and what didn't.

Sample questions:

- Who settled this community and what cultures did they bring with them?
- What are the visible signs of the cultures that shaped this community?
- What cultural stories or events have shaped the community's understanding of itself?
- What cultures have been devalued or suppressed?
- Have there been community controversies over cultural differences? What have people learned?
- Have there been times when the whole community has come together to celebrate its culture? What were they?
- What are the symbols of this community? How did they come about?

What to do with this knowledge:

- Plan and organize a cultural display in your library or school.
- Start an oral history project among students. Visit the website of the Cultural Wellness Center, www.ppcwc.org.

6 ISAIAH's Worldview

A broad, bipartisan citizen group skilled at tackling tough public problems shows how attention to the cultural and values dimensions of
issues can generate new power and energy.

O N OCTOBER 10, 2004, LESS THAN A MONTH BEFORE THE 2004
election, more than four thousand members of the ISAIAH group
gathered at the Roy Wilkins Auditorium in St. Paul to proclaim their
faith in democracy. ISAIAH is a multiracial, nonpartisan, economically
diverse organization with eighty member Protestant and Catholic congregations in the Twin Cities and its suburbs and in St. Cloud, a small
city fifty miles away.

The event testified both to the diversity of ISAIAH's membership
and the clout and effectiveness of the organization. A delegation came
from African American congregations in the St. Cloud affiliate, the
Great River Interfaith Partnership (GRIP), fresh from a successful campaign against racial profiling that had resulted in agreements with the
police department to curb the practice. Thirteen St. Paul congregations
celebrated their role in the selection of a new St. Paul police chief. St.
Paul ISAIAH had recently also pressed successfully for a Hmong-
speaking advocate on domestic violence in the police department.
Twenty-six member congregations in Minneapolis reflected on their

neighborhood outreach initiative, a series of discussions and one-on-one meetings with communities in the city to discover issues for action, launched the previous June. The eight congregations of ISAIAH's northwest suburban caucus publicized their success in preventing a growth-management plan under consideration by the planning commission, which in their view would have severely decreased the number of affordable housing units for low- and moderate-income families. Suburban church ladies mingled with inner-city residents. Fifteen hundred people came from Our Lady of Guadalupe, Ascension, Santo Rosario, and a dozen other Latino churches. More than forty state legislators were there, mixing with church bishops and business and labor leaders.

The mood was upbeat and also, often, challenging. "In one of the most divisive and contentious election seasons in recent history, there has been a tremendous focus by media and political parties on what divides us," read the press release. The group opened with an old internationalist hymn, "A Song of Peace" ("This is my home, the country where my heart is, / Here are my hopes, my dreams, my holy shrine, / But other hearts in other lands are beating, / With hopes and dreams as true and high as mine"). The program included music by South African partners. It adjourned to "America the Beautiful." The opening liturgy struck a note of unity: "People of God, we are not alone. God calls us out of our isolation into a powerful community where the values of our faith will be heard and will be seen. . . . We need no longer tolerate injustice, oppression, and exploitation." Scripture readings included a passage from the Koran. The design of the gathering was intended to illustrate public life itself—showing the possibilities for alliances among a mix of different interests and views. It also aimed to get out the vote for the coming election. Most importantly, it launched what leaders called a Faith in Democracy Campaign. The campaign addresses four issues intended to advance toward "a Minnesota with justice for all." At the gathering, plans were shared for a public education effort aimed at more state funding for schools. The public transportation campaign sought to "invest in a transportation system that works for all of us, including those without cars." The domestic violence initiative called for more funding to keep shelters open and provide services to victims. And, in anticipation of what would be a growing focus on immigration reform over the next two years, the civil rights for immigrants initiative called for passage of the Minnesota DREAM Act that would allow immigrant children to pay in-state tuition at public colleges and universities. It also called for public conversations across the state "to produce immigration reform that addresses systemic problems, inequities, and injustices." Jacqueline Belzer, Latino organizer for ISAIAH, followed up with dialogues.[1]

ISAIAH is characteristic of broad-based citizen organizations, as they are called, distinctive citizen groups with a populist flavor that have spring up over the last generation in cities across the country. I have heard similar issues and themes discussed in many such gatherings. Current generation broad-based citizen organizations of this type are gathered in four networks, including the Gamaliel Foundation, the Industrial Areas Foundation (IAF), the People Improving Communities through Organizing (PICO) national network, and the Direct Action and Research Training (DART) network. They see politics and organizing as about negotiating plurality, building public relationships across lines of difference, and pursuing social and economic justice.

In a tradition of community organizing that descends from the 1930s, broad-based citizen organizing has a progressive tilt. The organizations are also highly diverse. Members of such groups range from conservative Lutherans to liberal Unitarians in ISAIAH's network, the Gamaliel Foundation. Gamaliel stresses organizing in churches. In IAF or PICO, members may also include mosques, synagogues, trade unions, schools, or neighborhood groups. As of 2004, the four networks included 170 broad-based groups in thirty-three states, made up of several million families. All the networks have developed in roughly similar ways after the death of Saul Alinsky, the architect of modern community organizing, in 1972. The power and visibility of these groups in the organizing field has also generated many similar independent organizations.[2]

The Gamaliel Foundation has sixty affiliates in the United States and five in South Africa. It grew from the Contract Buyers League, an African American organization in Chicago fighting banks and savings and loan institutions that were using racially discriminatory practices. In 1986 the group established an organizing institute with a focus on "building power organizations in low-income communities." Barack Obama, the 2008 presidential candidate, worked as an organizer for Gamaliel in Chicago.

The effectiveness of ISAIAH over the years has come from the combination of several elements, also present in other citizen groups of this kind. It is intensely practical. ISAIAH and similar groups focus on what is feasible and winnable, grounded in a hard-headed assessment of what they call "the world as it is." They contrast this approach with a roseate view of "the world as it should be," a view they believe most social-change groups suffer from. Organizing is seen as the way to move in realistic ways from one toward the other. The emphasis on results was evident throughout the Faith in Democracy event's testimonials and stories of achievement. The booklet prepared for the meeting listed dozens of accomplishments large and small, from St. Matthew's successful closing of a drug house to what they call the Brownfields Story.

In 2002 and 2003, ISAIAH leaders organized an effort to leverage money for the cleanup of brownfields, polluted toxic sites in communities — over 3,000 acres of land that couldn't be used because it was too expensive for any city to clean it up. Leaders in ISAIAH member congregations organized the passage of a bill that committed $68 million toward the cleanup of Minnesota's brownfields. To put that in perspective, the state had only been spending $7.5 million on brownfield efforts. That $68 million is still being spent, and as of today has helped create over 10,000 living wage jobs in Minnesota. The ISAIAH leaders who made this happen learned a lot and are very proud. And we had a heck of a lot of fun in the process. We participated in a hearing at which "Moses" parted the "sea of red tape." We delivered bags of dirt with recipes attached for legislators to "turn polluted dirt into pay dirt." We held a press conference at which congregants in nuclear waste suits stood in a dump truck of dirt and unearthed "paychecks" representing the positive fiscal impact of brownfield development. And we organized city managers from around the state to come to the capitol and lobby on behalf of this effort for all of Minnesota.[3]

To achieve such results, ISAIAH takes a philosophical approach to politics and organizing, not an ideological or partisan one. Though their issue choices clearly tilt left, toward social justice, they don't divide the world into settled categories of allies and enemies. Nor do they build coalitions according to liberal-conservative divides. ISAIAH works with groups across the partisan spectrum on the issues that their members care about.

Instead of partisan politics, these groups stress values such as justice, human relatedness, and the sacredness of the person, not partisanship. They see everyone as full of contradictions and complexities; one's opponent today may well be a crucial ally tomorrow. Being excessively purist or overly principled in terms of whom one deals with is another blight common to the social action field, in their view. And reflecting such working principles, they have come to be highly skilled at developing public relationships, full of tension but also productive results, with establishment business and political leaders across the spectrum that community-organizing groups once simply targeted as the enemy.

Other groups in Minnesota have begun to pick up ISAIAH's emphasis on working through relationships, contrasted with either mobilizing approaches (demonizing an opponent and rallying the troops) or the informational approaches typical in professional life (sending out emails, flyers, reports, and studies). Peg Chemberlin, director of the Minnesota

Council of Churches, with three thousand congregations, says her organization learned from ISAIAH's focus on building relationships, rather than simply disseminating information.[4]

The effectiveness of such relationship-building work was evident in the large numbers of officials from both parties who showed up at the October gathering. Congressman Martin Sabo was there. So was House majority leader Steve Sviggum, a Republican, and many other office holders. Some had short speaking parts in the program.

ISAIAH also focuses on developing people's public leadership qualities and capacities, a focus I have seen elsewhere in this kind of broad-based citizen organizing. I am convinced this is the invisible key to their success. Doran Schrantz is ISAIAH's codirector. Schrantz, an energetic woman in her thirties, may be the youngest director of any such group in the country. She is engaging and intense, combining a theatrical flair (she once ran her own theater group in Chicago) with striking intellectuality. I asked her what had attracted her to organizing. "Love and power, that's what I saw in the organizers," she replied. "The idea that the path to my liberation was liberation of other people. The organizers were real; they were able to reach out and grab people not because they wanted to manipulate but because they loved them. They were saying, 'I want you to be who you can be.' I thought of that as freedom that only exists in certain spaces that have to be created. It's not a beer, or hanging out with friends. It's the kind of relationship with the world and with other people I was looking for."[5]

Many leaders and organizers in ISAIAH make similar observations about the intense focus on developing people's public potential. "ISAIAH involves a lot of people who are encouraged and given the space to use their natural talents to create something important," said Sarah Mullins, a case in point. Mullins, a young woman who works as a chemist for 3M, was in charge of the communications group for this event, far and away the largest and most important gathering in ISAIAH's history. She had no background in communications, but has a clear knack for developing messages and working with others. "Changing the public debate," not simply publicizing the event, was the innovative strategy that Mullins and her team developed. She was able to help several leaders write op-ed pieces, publish letters to the editor, and otherwise engage wider audiences in the underlying ideas of the event. Mullins described the emphasis on people's development in ISAIAH: "People care about issues, but also the people, not in a fluffy, caretaker way but in a 'we want you to develop as a person' way. The message in ISAIAH is, 'I don't know what you're going to be yet. You have to uncover that, in relationship to other people.'"[6] The booklet printed for the Faith in Democracy gathering stressed this human development dimension, calling it a way of living and a methodology. "ISAIAH is a way of 'living the faith,'" it says. Organizing "is a vehicle for the practice of a very specific methodology through which people can build the power necessary—individually and as a collective—to see their values realized in the world." The methodology includes what it calls "a set of attitudes and disciplines that are communicated through intensive training and practice. Attitudes about the importance of the work of the church, about acting with integrity, about being accountable to our commitments and holding others accountable, and about honesty with one another. Disciplines about prayer, building relationships, running effective meetings, mentoring others, and doing strategic planning."[7]

These themes are familiar to me from years of studying post–Alinsky citizen organizing. I appreciate the gritty practicality of such organizing work, the deep attention to human potential, the realization of the extraordinary possibilities in ordinary people, and their commitments to develop the power and possibilities of poor and working people in particular. I have been impressed with the relational and accountable cultures such organizations build and their successes in pressing for justice in difficult times, against the grain of the larger culture. ISAIAH has also added another dimension that I had never seen, what it calls its worldview. This is summarized in the lead paragraph of the *Faith in*

Democracy booklet. The statement reads, "ISAIAH is people of faith acting powerfully in the world, casting a stirring vision of a vital faith community that has the courage to declare, commit, and act upon a set of values. Those values will transform the dominant culture of despair, scarcity, and fear, replacing it with a vision of community, hope, and God's abundance for all people."[8]

Such broad, visionary, and ambitious language — transforming the dominant culture's values — is a clear departure from the pragmatic bread-and-butter issue language that characterizes the way such groups generally speak in the world, when they talk with politicians, for instance, or with the press, or with other groups. The difference in tone and language threaded through the Faith in Democracy gathering. "We believe in the sacredness of each individual," declared Pat Welter, a teacher from St. Cloud, describing their education initiative. "We believe that God has created us in community for our common good. And in a democracy, public schools are the heart of communities . . . democracy's cornerstone public institution."

Mary Lou Klas, a retired court judge and chair of the domestic violence task force, described the ravages of domestic violence and used similar language: "When we act together, we move from fear to hope; we transform ourselves; we are powerful." Jacqueline Belzer, from Church of the Ascension, who had been the key organizer behind the large turnout of Latinos, stressed human dignity in talking about the immigration effort, describing years of work as a housecleaner, without health insurance, benefits, or sick days, raising her daughter as a single mother, before beginning work with ISAIAH. "We all have the right to live a life that is dignified and just."

Grant Stevensen, pastor of St. Matthew's Lutheran Church in St. Paul, chair of the Clergy and Religious Leaders Caucus of ISAIAH, gave the keynote address, "A Battle for Who WE Are Going to Be." "Today there is a struggle going on for the soul of America," said

Stevensen. "Many people think that this is a struggle between Democrats and Republicans. . . . It is much larger than that. Is this country a
place where we live in fear of those who are different from us, or a
country of hope and opportunity for everyone?" Stevensen recalled the
discussions that had produced the ISAIAH worldview statement. "We
asked ourselves, who are we? What are our faith tradition's values?
And are those the values that are guiding the world today?" The answer
was a clear no, in his opinion. "People more and more are valued for the
amount of money they have and not for the creation of God that they
are." He said, "I'll be honest with you. I was starting to wonder how
many people even cared about the common good anymore. But I was
wrong. You care. It's all you've been talking about."⁹

The speech challenged political leaders and ISAIAH members alike.
"Why do some of our leaders think we can be so easily swayed by our
greed? Because we can be swayed and they know it," he said. "Some of
our leaders find that it's easier to appeal to our fears than to our
dreams . . . and let's tell the truth . . . there are days when we let them."
Stevensen then made a remarkable point about the nature of culture
change — it is about ourselves, as well as about the world. "This battle
for who we are going to be, for what kind of society we are going to create, goes on not just down at the capitol, but within our souls. It's always easier to think small, to stay at home, to be alone. But with you
here today I can believe that we can create a culture, a city, a state, even
a nation built not on fear but on hope."

The speech inspired the audience. Aneesa Parks, a teacher who
chairs ISAIAH's education committee, remembers, "I had heard him in
rehearsal and it still gave me chills." In Parks' view, the key message
was an invitation to be part of something big. "Grant said, 'Remember
that somebody invited you here. They invited you into something
larger.'" In her view, it gave clergy and others in ISAIAH a new way to
think about asking people to do something. "He was saying that if you

don't invite other people to be part of this, you're leaving them out of something that could change their life. The invitation is a gift, not a duty or a demand or a request."[10]

Returning to the Roots

In many ways ISAIAH's focus on culture change is a striking departure from the focus on bread-and-butter issues that broad-based organizing and other progressive citizen action groups inherited from the 1970s. In other ways, it returns to organizer Saul Alinsky's formative period, the populist movements of the 1930s and 1940s that were full of the language, strategies, and approaches of culture change and cultural organizing. In fact, this process of drawing on history as a resource is part of ISAIAH's worldview. "The politics of scarcity drives us to abandon the values we hold as people of faith and as citizens of this democracy," reads its vision statement. "However, when we look to our history as people of faith and at the history of people acting for justice in America, we see that there have been many times when ordinary people have stood together to make profound changes for the common good of all people."[11]

Today's broad-based organizing is rooted in this tradition of populist organizing. The contribution of Alinsky, who was widely seen as the architect of contemporary community organizing, was not in fact inventing community organizing, as is often imagined. Rather, Alinsky codified organizing lessons widely known by activists in the 1930s. His 1946 book *Reveille for Radicals* was a call to revive the movement without socialist baggage—Alinsky identified himself as a populist. Thus, Alinsky argued the need for organizers to listen to the communities where they are working, based on the insight that there are untapped democratic energies and potentials across partisan lines. "The starting of a People's Organization is not a matter of personal choice. You start with the people, their traditions, their prejudices, their habits, their attitudes, and all of those other circumstances that make up their lives." It meant seeing democratic potentials in a range of cultural communities. "To understand the traditions of a people is . . . to ascertain those social forces which argue for constructive democratic action as well as those which obstruct democratic action."[12] ISAIAH has begun to retrieve these traditions and approaches.

Developing a Worldview

ISAIAH's focus on culture change deepened in the year leading up to the Faith in Democracy gathering, especially through traveling dialogues held the summer before, but there were earlier developments to build on. One small congregation, Galilee Lutheran, in the suburban community of Shoreview, had held house meetings in 2002 and 2003 about the state of the world, as part of what they called an in-reach process, involving its members in reflection on what is happening in society, encouraging responsibility for doing something about negative trends, and developing the civic courage to speak and act, not simply to be a spectator. "We had discussed a lot the famous story of the woman murdered in New York in the 1960s while her neighbors watched, doing nothing," remembered Ron Peterson, church council president at Galilee who helped design the in-reach process. "We were determined not to be spectators like that."[13]

The discussions involved about sixty of the hundred members at Galilee in an intensive process, two hours of discussion a week for seven weeks. Eight or nine people met in different groups. They would begin with a question, a Bible verse, some things to think about, but generally the meetings were not highly structured. They touched a deep chord, breaking the silence in ways similar to what we have seen in the house meetings organized by Minnesota Works Together or that people have found in groups like Balance4Success in the southern suburbs. "People were dying to have an adult conversation about the state of the world," Peterson said. "It just kind of bubbles up when people have a comfortable space to talk." The conversations uncovered many concerns. "The lack of family time was a big thing," said Peterson. "It came up a lot. There was a sense of general malaise, that things in the society are not getting better. People said the culture is falling apart — morals, family structures, people getting hurt, consumerism."

While Galilee's discussions were feeding into ISAIAH, key figures in the organization were also ready for a new stage. "I never wanted to be in a monastery!" exclaimed Doran Schrantz, when I recounted conversations I had had with leaders in broad-based organizing in other networks. "I thought about organizing as a vehicle for human transformation, a process, not only an end. But equally it's about winning, and not just winning small fights but being part of a movement that can change the way we live together." Schrantz felt uneasy with what she thought was excessive timidity in the organizing field. "I believe the whole field is struggling with the question, Do we want to be engaged with major change or not?" She posed a series of questions about community organizing. "Do we want to be one of the groups that are going to change the country, or do we want to stay a monastery trying to survive the Dark Ages. It's kind of wonderful to be a monastery. But I want to unleash this power in the world."[14]

Dave Mann, a longtime progressive activist, cofounder of Minnesota Alliance for Progressive Action (MAPA), had been working with Richard Healey, a progressive philosopher well schooled in the theory and practice of 1930s cultural organizing. Healey and Mann worked with progressive groups around the country to help them develop worldviews that could be more compelling than a narrower focus on specific issues. Mann was married to Pamela Twist, then an organizer for ISAIAH. They began to discuss the idea of developing a worldview in 2003 with key leaders in the organization and found a good response. ISAIAH began to hold meetings with dozens of leaders to develop core values.

The worldview discussion was also prompted by a large goal organizers had set for themselves in 2003, in a meeting with colleagues from the national Gamaliel network. Paul Marincel, who had helped put ISA-IAH together in the 1990s and is now a national codirector of Gamaliel, and Jay Schmidt, ISAIAH's codirector with Doran Schranz, had pledged to organize a meeting with four thousand participants just before the 2004 election. "When they came back and told us, we were at first resistant. So were leaders. Many were angry. They asked, 'where the hell did this come from?'" remembers Schrantz. Both the discussions of the worldview idea and the potential of moving the work to another level of visibility and impact eventually convinced almost everyone. "We realized we couldn't do this by just doing more of what we were doing," Schrantz said. "We couldn't simply have more one-on-ones. We had to have more energy, more a sense of what we were about in the larger world. It was a problem to solve."

A key element in solving the problem and generating energy proved to be the traveling dialogues organized in 2004. Anessa Parks was an architect. "I had been listening to an NPR [National Public Radio] story about a guy who gave up his conventional life and wanted to have conversations with everyday people," remembered Parks. "He went to bars and coffeehouses and laundromats. He called them traveling dialogues. I thought, that's kind of what we're doing. Let's call it that." Schrantz and Parks made a plan for what the traveling dialogues might look like. In another national meeting, Parks committed herself to training thirty people and organizing discussions in fifty churches. ISAIAH ended up training thirty-three facilitators and holding dialogues in seventy-four churches.

"We structured them around the ideas of hope, abundance, and community, the core values that had come from the worldview discussions," said Parks. They were easy discussions to have. "All you needed to do was ask the first question, 'What do you see in the future of your children or grandchildren? What do you think about when you read the paper?'" People named many more fears than hopes. The meeting facilitator would point this out. "We would say, which of these things you mentioned are fearful, and which are hopeful?" She found that people easily recognized that they were talking mostly about fears. Parks asked, "What's the cost if we stay in this place of fear and our solutions come from that place?"

Then she changed the framework. She asked, "What if we saw things from a place of hope? What would the possibilities be then?" Facilitators found that this shift generated energy. "People would get excited," she remembered. It also proved an effective way to make the three core values, hope, community, and abundance, real to people, and ideas that leaders could articulate. "A few people felt a little shoved, but eventually everybody agreed that the shift is important. People realized we could be much more effective by talking about these values than simply talking issue by issue." It also was a different way of understanding the issues themselves. "'What would a hopeful solution look like for immigration?' we asked. 'Or education?'"[15]

The focus on worldview values has changed the conversation, according to organizers and leaders I have talked with in ISAIAH and also to leaders outside. "ISAIAH sounds less confrontational, more conversational," says Nora Slawik, a Democratic representative from Maplewood who has regularly interacted with the organization. She also tried out the language herself. "It really buoyed the crowd at the precinct caucuses," Slawik remembers. "It lifted people up. Politicians get too stuck in issues. But I think that people really want a value-based language. They can understand the difference between hope and fear. People are really experiencing fear these days. To talk about that fear, and that there can be an answer, gets a reaction."[16]

Because of its clout, because of its size, because of its intense focus on human development, and because of the power of a values language, ISAIAH seems poised to have significant impact on the public landscape of Minnesota in the next several years. Yet I believe that ISAIAH still is limited by its fairly conventional social justice framework.

Such a framework simply takes as a given the split between individual success and community commitments that is challenged by Atum

Azzahir. Thus, at the ISAIAH Northeast caucus roundtable on March 19, held at St. John the Baptist Catholic Church in New Brighton, I heard Myron Orfield outline disparities of income and education in the Twin Cities area. Orfield, director of the Institute on Race and Poverty, is a fine scholar of metropolitan disparities and a strategic partner of Gamaliel. He is also a frequent speaker at ISAIAH's meetings who has his own views on what to do. He gave his policy prescriptions, proposing that poor and minority kids from inner cities be dispersed to suburban schools in order to overcome the achievement gap on standardized tests, "in sufficiently small numbers so that the policy will not provoke counter reactions."[17]

Throughout his talk, I was struck by how much his approach is based on a scarcity model. It slights the profound cultural and learning resources of the sort that the Cultural Wellness Center cultivates in the Powderhorn and Phillips neighborhoods and with cultural communities, or that the Neighborhood Learning Community has developed on the West Side of St. Paul through its culture of learning (described in Chapter 8). It also ignores the cultural discontents at the heart of our fast-paced, fragmented, individualized, commercialized civilization, the same ones Balance4Success has been organizing about in the southern suburbs, or that Galilee discussions uncovered in Shoreview.

I found the leaders and organizers of ISAIAH generally open to discussing such questions. Jeanne Ayers, who organized the New Brighton meeting, decided to slow down the shift from values to issue development or policy prescriptions. "I know we have just begun to think about what our values of hope, community, and abundance mean in policy terms," she said. Sara Gleason, on the core ISAIAH leadership team, expressed her view that the focus on moving from isolation to community opened the door to new organizing on issues like family over-scheduling and the hypercompetitive cultures of the suburbs. "That's the kind of thing we never could have addressed without developing this worldview approach," she said.[18]

Mainly, the leaders and organizers see themselves as at the beginning of a new stage, unsure where it will lead but open to its development. Sue Eng, a Lutheran pastor who served on ISAIAH's staff for several years, believes that the worldview approach needs to challenge the organization to be as concerned about culture change in denominations "as we are about issues in the legislature." And Doran Schrantz argued that "we are really in a struggle now about what it means to be a power organization in this society, at this time. There are tensions between what we've inherited, what we're about, what we need to change, and how we relate to other constituencies. We've only done the first chapter. Now we're faced with the question, what does it mean?"[19]

The question of what it means to undertake a sustained, powerful, long-term effort to rebuild our communities at the same time we address public problems can be asked in a myriad of contexts. It will have many results. It is also possible, on the basis of the lessons from the pioneering work of active groups like the Cultural Wellness Center, Balance4Success, the ISAIAH group, and others, to begin sketching several shifts that it will entail: from spectatorship to powerful citizenship; from isolation to community; from information to wisdom; and from scarcity to abundance. The following chapters suggest something of what this might look like.

Sixth Civic Skill: Public Evaluation

Another skill that has proven essential in today's effective citizen efforts is public evaluation. Public evaluation helps citizen groups or communities learn from experience, expose tensions and conflicts in constructive ways, and become more public. They teach the vital lessons that mistakes and mishaps are inevitable—and can be a source of considerable learning and growth. They help people learn not to take such mistakes personally.

Public evaluation is different than an outside evaluator coming in to make a judgment, which may or may not be useful. Public evaluations are owned and done by the people involved. It is also different than the anonymous individual evaluation forms people sometimes fill out about an event or a meeting. Public evaluation is public—done collectively and openly in a discussion. Not everyone has to agree. They are to get an overall sense of what worked, what didn't, and what can be learned and done better.

Public evaluations should be done in terms of the goals and objectives that the group has agreed to, as individuals and collectively. The goal is to learn and to teach accountability to each other. It is a great skill to practice—rotate who leads the evaluation.

TIPS AND TOOLS

Facilitator: Have someone agree to lead the evaluation beforehand.

Ground rules: Create a time limit—say, five minutes at the end of a meeting—and brainstorm about other key rules (like don't interrupt, don't attack, and talk briefly), if public evaluations are new.

Recording: It is important to write down comments, on a board or flip chart. Find someone to do this.

Evaluation by goal: The evaluation leader lists the goals for the meeting or event, recognizing that goals are part of the larger process of ongoing collective work. Evaluation needs to reference what you were trying to accomplish in specific terms, but the most useful question is, "How did we do with our work?" This will elicit other thoughts and feelings about the meeting.

What worked? What can we learn? One simple way to evaluate is to say what worked and what didn't (or what could be done better). It is also often useful to do this in terms of process and content.

A rousing conclusion: The evaluation leader should refrain from offering opinions during the evaluation itself, but should make some overall comment on the meeting, the challenges facing the group, or the inspirations and lessons that came out of it.

7 Everyday Politics

Youth organizing shows the importance of learning a citizen-owned politics of empowerment and public work. The talents and energies of young people and young adults are crucial to the emerging civic movement.

TODAY, MANY PEOPLE FEEL LIKE SPECTATORS TO WHAT'S happening in the larger world. People almost everywhere, from inner-city neighborhoods to suburbs and rural communities, feel powerless to do anything about problems in major institutions and the larger culture. For the last twenty years, the Humphrey Institute's Center for Democracy and Citizenship (CDC) has worked with citizens and also with groups and institutions: schools, the state Extension service and community education, the Metropolitan Council, local governments, nursing homes, colleges, and others. Throughout, a central question has been how people shift from being spectators to being citizens. Such change in identity is the first key element in the shift from me to we. It involves identity change, in addition to new skills, knowledge, or values. Becoming a citizen means becoming a public person, an actor in the larger world. From the start, we knew that young people would play a central role in this shift.

I learned this as a young man in the freedom movement of the 1960s. I saw that when cultures have become full of fatalism and hopelessness, it is often only young people who break the cycle of despair. When black youth in the South developed courage and hopefulness about the possibility of change, they transformed adult cultures of defeatism and despair. Taylor Branch captures this in *Pillar of Fire*. In his account, the entire movement may well have turned on a fateful moment when Martin Luther King came around to accept the view of field staff members James Bevel and Diane Nash, who argued that allowing young people to march in Birmingham demonstrations in May 1963 was crucial. The adult African American community opposed continued demonstrations for fear of retaliation, based on decades of repression, and the movement might well have collapsed. When King agreed, thousands of teenagers and children began to participate, with dramatic results. "On the first day, nearly a thousand marching children converted the Negro adults," Branch writes. "The conflicting emotions of centuries played out on their faces until some finally gave way. One elderly woman ran alongside the arrest line, shouting, 'Sing, children, sing!'" The fatalism in the community dissolved.[1]

The Politics of Empowerment

Public Achievement has been the main vehicle that we developed at the Center for Democracy and Citizenship (CDC) to effect this change in identity from spectator to citizenship among young people. It involves teaching the skills and habits that accompany and sustain such identity change. Its core philosophy is captured in a song that Dorothy Cotton taught participants in the citizenship schools during the civil rights movement: "We Are the Ones We've Been Waiting For."

Public Achievement is based on cooperative team action on real-world problems and issues. Young people themselves choose the issues they want to work on and design and implement strategies of action. They are coached by older people, in most places young adults, who teach political and civic skills and concepts in teachable moments as the work progresses.

Public Achievement was launched by Project Public Life (soon to be the Center for Democracy and Citizenship) on May 24, 1990, at the Martin Luther King Center in St. Paul. About two hundred young people spent the day with teachers and community leaders. The launch was preceded by a series of twenty-one house meetings with teenagers, held in association with the newly elected mayor of St. Paul, Jim Scheibel. Although conventional wisdom in the United States held that youth were apathetic and unconcerned, it soon became clear that young people — every group we talked with — had major problems they worried about. These ranged from violence, teen pregnancy, drugs, gangs, and racism, to depression, lack of recreational opportunities, school reform, or lack of time with their families. Issues varied somewhat with area, class, and race. Concerns with gangs were much more common in inner cities, for instance. Yet many crossed geographic, racial, and income lines. Young people in every setting, for instance, expressed anger at school policies they felt were unfair, or at teaching approaches that failed to recognize and engage their interests and intelligence.

Young people in every group said that no one had ever asked what they could do to address these problems themselves. No one, in other words, had imagined that young people have the capacity (or interest) to act on the problems they are concerned about. The fact dramatized for me a disturbing feature of contemporary culture: young people are seen in passive roles, sometimes as consumers, sometimes as victims, sometimes as empty vessels in need of filling, sometimes as sentimental idealists, sometimes as foot soldiers in someone else's army. Rarely are young people conceived as creative, productive agents of change about issues they are themselves defining.

Other key aspects of Public Achievement came out of this early period, such as the concept of coaches (young people liked the idea of adults as coaches, more than any other role—advisor, teacher, mentor).

Young people also responded powerfully to the idea of a public world where they can interact with people outside their own community.

The flagship for Public Achievement was St. Bernard's K–8 elementary school in St. Paul, Minnesota. There, the principal, Dennis Donovan, now national organizer for Public Achievement, had undergone what he called a personal transformation through his involvement in SPEAC, a precursor to ISAIAH in St. Paul. Donovan saw Public Achievement as a way to teach students, who often voiced lack of purpose and despair, a new sense of their own power, along with hope, courage, and skills of effective citizenship.

Public Achievement was created as a contemporary citizenship school for young people and as an alternative to the protest politics that young people usually have seen as the alternative to electoral involvement. Public Achievement aimed at giving young people the opportunity to be creative political actors and social change agents themselves. In Public Achievement, teams choose what issues need to be addressed, what solutions might be, and how to pursue them. Moreover, particular issues are examples of the larger changes that need to take place if we are to build thriving communities and a democratic society.

A Tale of Two Playgrounds

The first story is about a group of young people at St. Bernard's school in the working-class North End area of St. Paul. In this case, Public Achievement teams of fifth, sixth, and seventh graders worked for four years to create a playground. They eventually succeeded, overcoming many obstacles. Joey Lynch, a leader in the teams, was recognized by Governor Jesse Ventura in his first State of the State address in 1999 as a "citizen prevailing against all odds."

Watching the work of the Public Achievement playground group unfold over the years, I know the rich civic and political learning that took place. Dozens of children were directly involved and the local school, church, and neighborhood were all affected. A number of students from James Farr's political science classes at the University of Minnesota were also involved as coaches and derived important learning from the experiences.

Teams were coached by adults who helped them develop achievable goals and learn political skills and political concepts. At St. Bernard's, several generations of teams worked on the issue. In order to succeed, teams had to turn neighborhood opinion around on the playground issue (neighbors had originally thought that a playground might be a magnet for gangs). They had to get the parish council on their side, negotiate zoning changes with city officials, and raise $60,000 from local businesses. To accomplish these feats, the children had to learn how to interview people, write letters, give speeches, and call people they didn't know on the phone. They had to learn about the culture, networks, and values of people in the neighborhood, and come to understand the views of adults they thought were mean and oppressive. They learned to negotiate, make alliances, raise money, map power, and do research.

Throughout, they liked describing their efforts as public work, sentiments suggested in the name the young people chose for the park, Public Achievement Works. Public work—defined as the ongoing efforts of a mix of diverse people who create things of lasting civic value—conveys the idea that young citizens can be co-creators of communities and the world, citizens today, not citizens in preparation. Public work can also be called everyday politics, and is a crucial way that a sense of generative power becomes integrated into lives and identities.

The playground effort showed the potential talent and political interests of young people. But the more typical experience that young people have with what is called "politics" is illustrated by a second story, this one about a young friend of mine, Daniel, who worked for the affiliate of a nationwide community-organizing network in a large urban area. A group of young people in the low-income neighborhood where Daniel organized told him they wanted to get a playground.

Daniel, who knew about the Public Achievement experience, wanted to see what they could do.

He approached the local organizing director for the citizen group. She was skeptical. "What does a playground have to do with power?" she asked. She feared that concentrating on a playground might detract from the upcoming mayor's race. She believed energy should go into mobilizing citizens for clearly progressive causes. Her conclusion was that Daniel could work with the teenagers on the playground issue only under certain conditions. He had to be able to "cut" the issue in a progressive way, which is organizing language for identifying a clear enemy and making sure most people agree. He had to figure out how it could be used to organize a protest.

As Daniel talked with the teenagers, he found that this approach did not make much sense. It wasn't likely to get a playground, even if they could find out which person in the Parks Department to target as the enemy. In any case, through the summer months, the organization became increasingly involved in the mayor's race. Daniel felt relief, and so did other staff. "Our organizing clay suddenly makes sense when poured into this mold," he commented. "Some camaraderie is really beginning to creep into walls that seemed to house folks who talked about quitting nearly every day. Campaigning is all about numbers, mobilizing the base and turning out the regulars. We don't even pretend to develop leaders or build anything sustaining. We just go out and get the numbers."[2]

This kind of episode is all too common. The highly scripted, manipulative styles of work in many activist groups burn out huge numbers of young adults. Those not burned out can become locked into a view of politics as simply ideological warfare, far from the practical public work and relationship building across lines of difference needed to revitalize civic life.

In Public Achievement, teams address a large range of issues, including teen suicide, racial profiling, violence, and school curriculum.

A variety of evaluation studies often show remarkable accomplishments and, even more important, deep change in young people's sense of themselves in the world and their relationship to the world. This is especially true where Public Achievement is more than a "program"—in places where it is integrated into school or community cultures as a different way of engaging young people that affects other activities as well. In 2007 about three thousand young people were involved in Public Achievement in more than eighty sites in a number of American communities. Public Achievement has also spread to Northern Ireland, South Africa, Scotland, Turkey, Palestine, Israel, Poland, Moldova, Ukraine, Serbia, Romania, Macedonia, and other Balkan countries.

Public Achievement and Young Adults

In the last several years, Public Achievement has begun to involve young adults and college students directly in their own team projects. They apply skills of everyday public-work politics themselves, rather than simply coaching younger children. This has proven effective, and it also opens a window into the issues, discontents, and passions that roil their generation. Several leaders in the Public Achievement network outside Minnesota have played key roles in this process, including Eric Fretz at the Denver University and Adam Weinberg, former vice president of Colgate University in New York.

Minneapolis Community and Technical College (MCTC) helped lead the way. With support from President Phil Davis and Vice President Lois Bollman, its urban teacher program and parks and recreation programs integrated Public Achievement into their core curriculum. Emphasizing skills drawn from broad-based organizing such as naming and using power, clarifying and acting on self-interests, understanding the difference between public and private relationships, and navigating urban environments, the programs now prepare students from urban communities to become democratic change agents in those communities, citizen teachers and citizen recreation workers. One semester they do their own team projects, and then coach at several area schools the next.

Michael Kuhne, on the MCTC faculty, observes that making concepts such as free space and everyday politics come to life is often difficult. Usually, the teacher "teaches" and the student "learns." Free spaces are not bestowed. "It is not simply a question of the instructor declaring that the classroom is a free space and circling up the desks (though that is a start) . . . free space is created and re-created collaboratively."[3]

For all the challenges, the Public Achievement approach has proven to be a civic and political pedagogy with strong appeal to young adults. "I recall that in the beginning of the semester, Dennis Donovan asked me if I wanted power. I said, 'no,' because I did not know what to do with it," recounted Mona Abdel-Kerim. Her views changed. "Now I want the power because I believe I have the ability to help others who want to make a difference." Tami Giinther tied power to her future career. "As a future teacher I can't stress enough how important it is to be confident with the power one has; otherwise the students and coworkers will see that the teacher can't handle power." Lisa Staplin argued that people need to be realistic about gaining power. "It will be good for students to learn that there are many levels of power, and that while they may have little power on their own, if they can find others with the same interests as a group they have much more power and can really affect changes in their world."[4]

As with younger children, MCTC students also came to have strongly positive associations with politics. "I had to present my issue in such a manner that would make it stand apart from my other classmates' presentations, yet make my issue sound attractive," Danielle Peterson said. "The intricacies of language, public speaking capabilities, creativity, and—really—charm came into play in this political act." Many also generalized to their future careers. "It has advanced my training as a future teacher by opening up my mind to where politics takes place," said

Jena Vue. "I use to think very narrowly and naïvely that politics only takes place in the government. Learning about this core concept has given me the understanding that politics is everywhere and that a classroom environment does explore politics."

Similarly at the University of Minnesota, college students who have begun to do Public Achievement often remark on a new sense of power and willingness to build relationships across differences. Public Achievement came to the university through integration of its civic pedagogy into the core curriculum of the well-established Leadership Minor, involving several hundred students from different departments. "When students in the second year leadership class began to do Public Achievement, it was like they woke up," said June Nobbe, director of student development and leadership at the university. "I could see in their faces how much they loved learning the skills of powerful, effective action."[5]

This work has also highlighted the cultural concerns about eroding community identified by Kelly Heskett's group. In the fall of 2005, the Leadership Minor, the Center for Democracy and Citizenship, and students in Jim Farr's political science class held several house meetings with undergraduates. These exposed strong feelings that the University of Minnesota culture fragments and isolates students into bubble cultures, treats students through the lens of adult stereotypes, and offers few free spaces where students can form meaningful, deep relationships either among others of their age of different backgrounds or with older adults. Students voiced the strong desire to see such discussions continue and spread.

Donovan began to work with a core group of fifteen undergraduates who soon named themselves SCOPE, the Student Committee on Public Engagement. They planned and organized a university-wide Civic Summit for March 30, 2006, to which they personally invited leaders from diverse student groups, staff, and faculty, ranging from the Carlson School of Management to the Institute of Technology, from the athletic department to campus Democrats and Republicans.

To prepare, the group developed a vision statement. The event, students declared, was intended to be a strategic meeting with student leaders, faculty, administration, Public Achievement participants, and others. The purpose was "to bring together groups and individuals who are working toward a more civically involved community in order to collaborate and create a unified message. Many people are working on similar projects but few are making these resources known and available. In doing so . . . we can contribute to the university community, this state and country, as well as the world by synthesizing our power and passions."[6]

More than seventy people participated. The Civic Summit included three hours of house meetings in which diverse groups discussed what they valued about the University of Minnesota, what were obstacles to building a sense of community and engagement, and what could be done to change things. In the meeting as well as subsequent interviews with Scopers, as they call themselves, I was struck by the depth of the students' passion for rebuilding a relational culture of community. Their passion has both public and private dimensions.

In public terms, the organizing skills they have learned in Public Achievement and related efforts like SCOPE have sometimes changed or deepened the ways they relate to their friends and fellow students. Russ Lyons, one of the organizers of the spring 2006 fraternity rush, became active in MPIRG, the student activist group, after being politically "activated" the year before by attending Camp Wellstone, a training center that continues the populist tradition of the late senator Paul Wellstone and his wife, Sheila. I had wondered about his comment at the Civic Summit that "oppression language doesn't work with most of my generation." I asked what he meant.

"In my fraternity, the oppression language really turns people off. A lot of the Greeks come from small towns or suburbs where they've never known how to deal with different races. One of the things that really bothered me was their racist jokes." Lyons began to call them racist. One fraternity brother told him it made him think. But for others, it was a prod to go to the Internet and find more jokes to make him upset. "It only shut them down, it didn't open them up," he said. "So I decided to try the one-on-one approach I'd learned from Public Achievement. I had really deep conversations. People began sharing parts of themselves that I'd never heard before, and I'd lived in the house for more than two years."[7]

Laila Davis, an astute graduate student at the Humphrey Institute, sees strong personal dimensions to young people's interest in building relationships. In a conversation with Petra Duecker, a leader in SCOPE and many other campus efforts, she realized that older adults have sustained relationships with families and with coworkers that can no longer be taken for granted. The younger generation lives in a more turbulent time, when virtual communities like MySpace create ephemeral relationships. Today, though students yearn for depth in relationships, they also have less experience with them so they need skill-building experiences that often come from public life. "The younger generation's need [for public life] may partially reflect a cultural shift in our society over the years," Davis argues.[8]

As Davis and Duecker suggest, turbulence at home interacts with turbulence in the mass culture. The Pew Research Center found in April 2005 that "roughly six in ten Americans say they are very concerned over what children see or hear on TV, in music lyrics, video games, and movies." Bill Stephney, cofounder of the rap group Public Enemy, observes the normalization of crime, drug use, and prostitution in gangsta rap in the mass culture. In 2003, a study of teenagers in twelve countries by researchers Melvin and Margaret DeFleur concluded that "the depiction of Americans in media content as violent, of

American women as sexually immoral, and of many Americans engaging in criminal acts has brought many of these youthful subjects to hold generally negative attitudes" toward Americans.[9]

In this climate, young adults who are serious about building relationships have to overcome the fact that the culture undermines such relationships in many ways. The struggle is not only to learn relational skills but also how to resist the seductions of a mass culture that conveys contempt for depth in relationships—and how to change the culture. Several undergraduates described aspects of cultural turbulence both in their growing up and at the University of Minnesota.

Amy Jo Pierce, a student government leader and a University of Minnesota student trustee, says she grew up in a dysfunctional family, raised by her father because of her mother's troubles with drugs. They were poor but close-knit. "There would be weeks when there wasn't much food; I started working at fifteen; but what stood out for me was how my family worked together. My dad showed us unconditional love. My grandparents and aunts and uncles really supported us." The University of Minnesota was a shock. "When I first came to the U, I thought, this school is way too big. It's easy to get lost." She questioned everything, including her faith, and adopted the party lifestyle of those around her. But throughout she slowly made connections, went back to church, joined a sorority, Kappa Alpha Theta, and the student government, where she eventually became vice president. "It was awesome when I got to be vice president. I realized I can't be seen as a party vice president, I have to be seen as a serious person."[10]

Pierce was part of the Leadership Minor and loved Public Achievement. "It helped me think about leadership differently. Leadership is not for the glory of myself. My position is not as important as how I'm helping other people." What she liked was the idea of helping other people develop their own power. "The most important thing about Public Achievement is that it makes you feel like you are a worthwhile and valued person. And that you learn how to consciously build relationships." She brought these lessons to student government, helping committee chairs to learn a more collaborative, relational, empowering style. And she sees groups like SCOPE and other organizing efforts as a means to creating a more relational culture of community at the University of Minnesota that crosses party lines. "At this point, the U can just intensify bickering between people."

Pierce is conservative, and she especially disliked the sweeping judgments she feels some faculty members make. "If a professor is standing in front of their class and saying it's okay to be polarized, that Republicans are horrible, people come to think politics is just about fighting." Public Achievement organizing, in her experience, is about learning how to work together as a diverse group. "The challenge for SCOPE," according to Pierce, "is how the group can focus on making change in the campus culture, in the spirit of Public Achievement. We need to make a lot of changes, like policy change so faculty focus more on teaching. It is all about creating safe places to express oneself and groups like SCOPE need to uphold that tradition."

Blake Hogan came up with the original idea of SCOPE and gave the opening speech at the Civic Summit. Hogan also had challenges growing up. He was raised by a single mother in the Twin Cities suburb of Blaine. In high school, Hogan was a star athlete, on the student council, in the honor society, and in other groups. He said his public involvements had a lot to do with "coming from an unstable family." They were "a safe haven, a comfortable place to be. It was fun, you were with your friends. It also helped with your resume." He loves America, and deeply identified with the traditions and values of his grandfather's generation, which built public-works parks and public buildings in the CCC and WPA, and fought for freedom in World War II. "Here I am, a kid from a family with an alcoholic dad, a diabetic mom, and no money, but I have had the chance to really be something if I am willing to get off my ass and work for it."[11]

Patriotism for Hogan is linked to what he calls "kingdom work," a concept that comes from his faith. Both kingdom work and patriotism are about "learning to give of yourself to a cause that's greater than yourself, to reach out and touch other people" in ways that make a difference. He doesn't think there is enough of that today. "We're Minnesota nice, and often times we don't have the courage to be real. Most people are afraid to step up because they don't think they can do it, or because they have yet to be invited to create positive change, or it's because they have not had the proper coaching, support, and mentoring to realize their potential." He believes that President Bush "had the opportunity to unite both the country and the global community following the tragedy of September 11 but faltered due to a narrow vision and inadequate leadership." SCOPE represents for Hogan a grassroots opportunity, "a vehicle to be a positive change agent in an ever changing culture, simply put."

In a Public Achievement project, Hogan worked with Amir Pinnix to begin a mentorship program at a high school. The project itself was a lesson in everyday politics. "We had our own ideas and goals—life skills, financial aid, and applications and tours of colleges, in sessions spread over ten weeks. The students weren't too excited about the ten week program idea. They wanted more personalized interaction and help, so we came to a compromise." Hogan also developed a close friendship with Pinnix that he believes will last his whole life. "One of the key things about this experience has been developing relationships with real people who are trying to do something."[12]

Pinnix was a running back on the University of Minnesota football team, the Golden Gophers. He grew up in Newark, in an African American community, with a single mother. The neighborhood was rough, but his extended family was very supportive, especially his grandmother and grandfather. His grandfather is a stonemason who works with a crew. "He didn't say much, but the guys had so much respect for him. I watched how he influences people by telling them what to do in a calm, subtle way." His grandmother was the outspoken one.

All his family conveyed values. "My mother instilled some great values in me. Keep God first, value your family, value your relationships. Those are the values I have today. That's how I made it though."

Pinnix embodies such values; he can be called a citizen athlete, with a deep sense of the authority and the responsibility that comes from being a high-profile football player. Through him, the concept of citizen athlete has begun to spread in Minnesota's athletic programs. "It's a big responsibility when I go home because a lot of kids know me athletically." He uses his prominence to challenge them. "I say, what's going on? What are you doing to help out? You have to get an education." Pinnix tells the story of a young kid, seven or eight, who came up to his car. "Yo, give me a dollar," the boy said.

"What?" said Pinnix.

"Ain't you the dude who play for Minnesota? Let me get a dollar."

"What are your grades like?" Pinnix asked.

"Man, I got Cs."

"I said, 'When I come back home, if you get straight As and Bs, I'll give you $20. And you take that and you make it useful. You help your people out.' I was trying to teach him to value your community." Pinnix concluded, "You know, the next time I came home that boy came up with his report card and he had made straight As. It really affected me."

Pinnix gave the final speech to the Civic Summit. He is a student of public speaking. Growing up he had studied many black leaders who spoke powerfully. "Whenever one spoke who had a powerful impact on the community, I would look and listen to their style." He studied Martin Luther King, Malcolm X, Amiri Baraka, a poet from Newark, and most recently Barack Obama. "I listened to tapes, I watched the Discovery Channel. I also listened to my minister and would see how he interacted with the congregation."

I asked what he had learned. "How to stand your ground and ask people, in a respectful way, to pay attention," he replied. "And how to inspire." Pinnix's speech illustrated how much he has learned. He got a standing ovation at the Civic Summit. In his speech Pinnix called for culture change at the university, using the image of bringing back the front porch to symbolize a relational culture. The front porch "is where it all starts," he said. "You get to know people. You socialize. You go off and do public work. But it all starts with the front porch."

Behind him as he spoke was a mosaic of front porch images from Alabama, where his family still owns land, outside Selma. He also drew on experiences in Newark. "There were a lot of front porches," he said. "People hung out on the front porch, day and night. They would talk about everything, from sports to what was going on in the world. The kids listened. We found out we had a lot of wise people in our community."

Learning the skills and ideas of power has led these students to believe that they can significantly influence the culture of the University of Minnesota. Where it will develop, how much they will do, is still an open question. But they have many allies in this work, at the university and far beyond it.

Seventh Civic Skill: Taking Action

Action can be usefully distinguished from activity—busyness, or the mindless proliferation of things to do. Our world drowns in activity. Action is thoughtful collective effort informed by understanding different self-interests and power relationships. It is based on prioritizing what is most important to start with. It is prepared with care. We need a lot more action. Another way to describe action is thinking strategically and carefully about what is important. The civic skills described in the preceding chapters can be understood as preparation for action on your issue or public project.

Below are some tips for learning to engage in action, not activity.

TIPS AND TOOLS

Develop a small team: You need people to work with if you want to be successful, people you can strategize and brainstorm with. A team should include people who are passionate about the issue, but also people with diverse strengths.

Figure out the rules: Every setting has a set of rules, principles, ways of acting, "the way things are around here." Sometimes they are open, but most are hidden and informal. For instance, one community principle or reality might be that people don't like to go to meetings. In this case, a key question to think through with your team is, how can meetings be designed to meet people's self-interests?

Make your rules: Develop your team's own rules of action and accountability.

Develop your mission and vision: Having a short, clear statement of what you are trying to achieve—a mission statement—and how it relates to your longer-term vision of what you would like to see is an important step.

Name the obstacles: A realistic discussion and listing of potential barriers to meeting your goals are always an important part of preparation. Many barriers and obstacles will only become apparent as you take action.

Research: Figure out what you need to know and how to find it out.

Timeline: Make a rough timeline for when you want to accomplish what—and recognize that this is likely to change as you take action.

One-on-ones: Make a plan for an initial round of one-on-ones about who can help you map interests and power, who might provide important information, who might be allies.

Prioritize: Figure out what is most important to do first.

8 From Isolation to Neighborhood Communities

A neighborhood learning community demonstrates the importance of physical places to the education of children. The group revives the traditions of St. Paul's old West Side, where children learned from neighbors, as well as from teachers in schools. The tradition also reconnects schools with neighborhood life.

"Enlighten the people generally, and tyranny and oppressions of body and mind will vanish like evil spirits at the dawn of the day."
THOMAS JEFFERSON

AMERICANS TODAY NEED TO REMEMBER THE PURPOSES of education envisioned by early educators. Benjamin Rush, a founding figure in American education, argued that public schools were the crucial bulwark against tyranny. "Where learning is confined to a few people, we always find monarchy, aristocracy, and slavery," he wrote in 1786. In Thomas Jefferson's view, the purpose of schools was educating public citizens and leaders who were examples of talent and virtue — as concerned about the common good and community life as they were about their own individual achievements and successes. This is more easily said than done.[1]

The problem is that nonprofessional citizens have become peripheral to formal education over the last generation. As this has happened, the civic mission of schools—educating for community concern as well as individual success—has been weakened. A central focus of the Cultural Wellness Center in Minneapolis is showing how to restore the connection between community and learning by showing the importance of cultural and community ties to human health and growth—and by drawing on the deep ties between community and education in African American and other cultural traditions. The Neighborhood Learning Community on the West Side of St. Paul has largely the same goal.

Taking the Public out of Public Schools

Since the 1960s, formal education, like many other institutions, has increasingly pushed parents and community residents to the sidelines. David Mathews, president of the Kettering Foundation, has argued that "the public as a real force in the life of schools was deliberately and systematically rooted out. Citizens were replaced with a new group of professionals, true guardians of the public interest, there to do what it was assumed citizens couldn't or wouldn't do." Peter Levine documents this pattern with statistics. For example, in 1960, membership in PTAs was 45 percent of all families with children in school. By the early twenty-first century it was less than half that figure.[2]

As a result, all the confident proclamations about programs and pedagogies designed to reduce the so-called achievement gap between poor and minority children and the middle class neglect the civic dimensions of defining accountability. As Mathews summarized the Kettering Foundation's research, "When citizens think about accountability they are particularly concerned with the moral commitments of educators, not just their professional or technical competence. . . . Studies show that people value teachers who can encourage and inspire, who can make learning come alive, who are inventive in their classrooms, and who are patient in one-on-one relationships with students." Overall, said Mathews, "citizens are looking for more than data from schools. . . . They want to know what kind of people their youngsters are becoming as well as how they are doing academically." In contrast, reform measures like No Child Left Behind emphasize formal teacher credentials and student test scores. Civic education, both formal and informal, has experienced dramatic decline.[3]

Anthropologist Annette Lareau explored this split between community and civic values and schools in her study of what she calls the "cultural logic" of poor and working-class families as compared to educators and high-achieving middle-class families. Today's educators, whether in suburbs or inner cities, reflect what Lareau calls "a dominant set of cultural repertoires about how children should be raised" that stress "concerted cultivation." These are the values of the highly individualistic, competitive, and achievement-oriented middle class—the same values that are creating discontent in southern Twin Cities suburbs. In contrast, "for working-class and poor families, sustaining children's natural growth is viewed as an accomplishment." For these families, clear boundaries exist between child and adult activities. There is a belief in the need for children to do things on their own, an emphasis on relationships with family and friends, and little stress on children's individual educational development.

Lareau's descriptions could have come straight out of the discussions that Balance4Success has had with families in Apple Valley. "In the middle class, life was hectic. Parents were racing from activity to activity. . . . Children's activities determined the schedule for the entire family. . . . Adults' leisure time was absorbed by children's activities." In contrast, though working-class and poor families felt much more economic strain, "children's lives were more relaxed and, more importantly, the pace of life was slower. Children played with other children outside of the house. . . . Some children had organized activities but they were far fewer than in middle-class families."[4]

On St. Paul's West Side, a strong coalition has formed to combine educational accomplishment with community life. In doing so, an abundance of hidden learning resources have surfaced.

The West Side was the Ellis Island of the Midwest, gateway to America for generations of immigrants. For years, the *West Side Voice*, the community newspaper, featured a highly popular history column called West Side Story, with characters and vignettes from earlier days of immigrant settlement. More than sixty murals have been painted on neighborhood buildings honoring civil rights heroes and local community activists, as well as street scenes and different ethnic traditions.

The ethnic mix on the West Side has changed over the decades, as Jewish refugees from Eastern Europe gave way to new waves of immigrants from Mexico, Southeast Asia, and East Africa. Now, residents of European descent are in the minority. The Latino population rose from 21 percent in 1990 to 33 percent in 2000. On the corner of Cesar Chavez Street and State Street, El Burrito Mercado stocks spices and fruits that recall the open-air markets of Mexico, offering groceries along with a restaurant, bakery, and deli. A Mexican Aztec dance group, Danza Mexica Cuauhtemoc, stages productions in the plaza outside. Today, 78 percent of public school students in the neighborhood are racial minorities.[5]

Some community traits remain unchanged over the years. Poverty continues to characterize parts of the neighborhood. And both middle-class and low-income people on the West Side have experienced troubling cultural trends. Like Apple Valley, if in different ways, the West Side has struggled to preserve community life.

Many dynamics have contributed to the erosion of civic life. By the 1990s, gangs were a growing problem in the area. Many nonprofits had come to see residents as needy clients, not as problem solvers and builders of the community. These changes were reflected in physical ways. For instance, Neighborhood House, no longer the anchoring institution of the neighborhood it had once been, had lost the meeting notices, pictures, and other distinctive features of the West Side and its diverse ethnic cultures that once made it a vibrant community center.

In addition, nonprofit organizations were battling each other for funding dollars, a pattern fed by local foundations which use evaluation methods that measure the number of clients in a program, not its civic impact. Collaboration among groups on the West Side had sharply declined. Many nonprofit organizations felt little identification with the neighborhood as a whole. All of this, in turn, reflected individualist values of achievement and personal success, detached from community life.

Schools both reflected this dynamic and helped to create it. On the West Side, like other places, the idea of the neighborhood school had sharply declined. School buses took children from the West Side to seventeen different schools across the city. In addition, a wide gulf had opened between neighborhood and school cultures. "There's a sense that when a community person comes, [school officials think] what do you really want?" said one community organizer. "There's a lot of distrust." Few local teachers lived on the West Side, and many knew little about what was happening in the area. [6]

Yet over the past decade, this pattern of separating people, organizations, and schools from the life of the West Side has begun to turn around. For instance, West Side images have returned to the walls of Neighborhood House. One can also hear a much stronger identification with the neighborhood from nonprofit staff and many teachers. There are visible early signs of a shift from isolation to community.

Community building today requires conscious organizing around concrete issues that tap into diverse interests. In the case of the West Side the catalyst for change is the Neighborhood Learning Community (NLC). It has become a model across the city and beyond for reconnecting communities and education and in the process helping revitalize neighborhood life.

The NLC is a network of people and organizations on the West Side working to strengthen learning opportunities for children. Its goal is to create a culture of learning in the neighborhood, drawing on diverse neighborhood resources in which all share a sense of ownership. As a recent report, *A Community Alive with Learning*, puts it, the NLC is based on the premise that "children's learning will improve if they grow up in a neighborhood with a culture of learning—one rich in learning opportunities, contexts, and expectations." This means a widely shared understanding that "the neighborhood is a place dense with relationships, rich with history and memories, and alive with learning the skills, values, and aptitudes needed for an interdependent globalized world." It also means a set of norms: "Everyone is expected and invited to be a teacher, a learner, and a co-creator of the common good."[7]

A Copernican Revolution

The goal of creating a culture of learning throughout a whole neighborhood is in line with recent research that ties children's academic development to their social development. It also goes against powerful trends. A growing body of scholarship demonstrates that children do far better in both academic and social terms in settings where parents, community groups, and schools collaborate and where there is appreciation for influences from outside the school and classroom. This scholarship shows the wisdom of citizen efforts in diverse settings where people are seeking balance in children's lives.

Laurence Steinberg examined student achievement in a wide range of settings and experiences in upper-middle-class, working-class, and lower-income schools. He and his research team discovered that while schools are important, time in school is simply one of many influences—and not the most important. What takes place in homes, peer groups, and neighborhoods is crucial for educational success and continuing interest in education. He argues that most educational reform efforts fail because they do not take into account the larger community context. Thus, he proposes that it is imperative to put new emphasis on experiences and places beyond the classroom. "No curricular overhaul, no instructional innovation, no toughening of standards, no rethinking of teacher training or compensation will succeed if students do not come to schools interested in and committed to learning."[8]

Visionary educational leaders understand these challenges. Elona Street-Stewart, the first Native American to be elected to a school board in a major Minnesota city and now chair of the St. Paul school board, argues that schools need to "shift the power and the control." In her view, "We need to listen to street corner conversations and turn traffic flow around. Instead of community coming into schools, [educators] need to go out to the community," becoming deeply familiar with and connected to neighborhood institutions, networks, and cultures.[9]

The dilemma is that such findings and insights run up against long-developing trends. As democratic education scholar Nick Longo has observed, "School centered approaches have dominated educational reform movements for the past century." Longo points out that conventional parent-involvement programs are school-centric. Parents (and other community residents) participate on the terms of the schools, with little opportunity to initiate, decide, or shape learning opportunities themselves. Education writer Dennis Shirley, analyzing community organizing by the Industrial Areas Foundation in Texas that has turned around the performance of dozens of schools, observes that conventional parent-participation approaches assume "an uncritical stance of parents toward the dominant culture of the school."[10]

To create educational reform that negotiates this gap and builds community in the process requires developing the power of families and involving them in the co-creation of educationally enriching activities. It also requires making schools and teachers far more connected to and respectful of relational values, neighborhoods, and ethnic and immigrant cultures across classes and incomes.

Culture change in the context of community cannot be accomplished by conventional political or professional approaches. Transferring children from low-income communities to supposedly high-achieving suburban schools simply assumes that the middle-class individualistic achievement culture is the ideal. Conservative approaches that offer low-income and minority children the option of leaving public schools through private school vouchers may benefit those who do it, but also neglect the work of reconnecting schools with civic life.

Traditional professional strategies do not work to create such culture change. The information-based approaches common in professional settings, where parents and educators are given research findings and reports, have little potential to engage families' interests, develop families' power, or create substantial relationships between schools and their surrounding communities. Traditional social-service program approaches deliver educational enrichment experiences to students conceived of as largely passive clients, not as creative agents who have potentially rich cultural resources to offer. As Longo points out, "Developing a neighborhood culture of learning counters prevailing trends and invites non-experts to participate in education reform." It is a "citizen centered model . . . that asks experts to . . . be on tap not on top." The challenge is that "this constitutes several paradigm shifts: seeing ordinary people as producers, not consumers; actors, not spectators; and teachers, not students." Jerome Stein, an educational scholar with rich experiences in immigrant and minority communities, adds that such a shift amounts to a Copernican Revolution. It means understanding that schools need to orbit around communities and families, not the other way around.[11]

Organizing the Neighborhood Learning Community

The Neighborhood Learning Community began in 2001 with a community dialogue among fifty West Side residents from different cultural and income backgrounds, along with representatives of different organizations. They asked, "How can we organize across the neighborhood to become a culture of learning?" Several ingredients made the West Side especially fertile ground.

The idea of communities and their diverse institutions claiming authority and power over children's learning and education is an old Minnesota tradition. Indeed, the link between education and the civic life of communities based on the sense that whole communities, not simply schools, are the responsible agents, is reflected in a series of pioneering Minnesota policies such as community education, service learning, and early childhood family education. This tradition was especially vibrant on the old West Side, with places like Neighborhood House and the Riverview Library, both of which sponsored extensive reading and learning projects among immigrants in the early decades of the twentieth century. Such history created rich resources to build on in organizing for a new culture of learning.

Some had begun consciously to reconnect with these traditions. For instance, Riverview Library, founded in 1917, began in the late 1980s under the leadership of Mary Margaret Sullivan to revive older practices of directly engaging new immigrants — in this case immigrants from Southeast Asia, Central and Latin America, and Africa. Library workers went into the community instead of waiting for immigrants to come to the library. It built sustained relationships with community groups. And it positioned itself as a vital information commons. "All of the traditional models of services don't work anymore when you're working with communities new to the American public library system," said Andrea Moerer, who headed the community engagement effort. "Just sending out flyers and having newspaper articles in English doesn't work." Sullivan believes that as a result, "We had to become a part of the fabric of the community. And that was the goal."[12]

Riverview Branch Library was an early leader in the Neighborhood Learning Community. Appreciation for new immigrant cultures as part of the organizing mix was also considerably enhanced by the Jane Addams School for Democracy, which played a catalytic organizing role. The Jane Addams School is a learning and public-work partnership that consciously renews the traditions of places like Neighborhood House and its sister institution, Hull House in Chicago. Like the earlier settlement houses, the Jane Addams School seeks to incorporate new immigrants and their cultures as dynamic resources in an evolving democratic society.

The Jane Addams School began as a partnership on the West Side of St. Paul with Hmong, Latino, and East African communities. It was co-founded in 1996 by Nan Skelton, codirector of the Center for Democracy and Citizenship, and Nan Kari, at that time director of faculty development at the College of St. Catherine, working with John Wallace, a faculty member in the philosophy department at the University of Minnesota, and Sandy Fuller, on the staff of Neighborhood House. From its beginning, the Jane Addams School included elements of an organizing approach. It has a strong emphasis on relationship-building, not one-way or didactic educational approaches. College students who participate go through an orientation that teaches them that they are members and participants, not students doing service projects. New immigrants prepare to pass the citizenship test with native-born U.S. citizens, usually students, in learning pairs that are highly relational. Moreover, each of the several learning circles that meet Monday and Wednesday nights (Hmong, Spanish, and East African, as well as children's and teen circles) has cultural exchange discussions. These include topics that range from family patterns to health and wellness or the meaning of citizenship.

Many organizing projects have emerged from the Jane Addams School, from working on immigration issues to school reform and neighborhood improvement. A continuing emphasis has been civic literacy, with attention to public leadership development in such skills as public speaking, understanding other's interests and backgrounds, and mapping the political environment. The Jane Addams School has also had extensive overlap with Public Achievement, which has offered opportunities for students at the West Side's Humboldt High School to take on community projects.

The overall philosophy at the school stresses that "everyone is a teacher, everyone is a learner," and the reciprocal, interactive quality of the Jane Addams School often has strong impact on participants. Exchange and learning also mean different things to different people. For immigrant youth, for instance, it often provides resources for forming more complex identities, balancing ethnic traditions with American culture. "I came to the States when I was very little, and my parents don't talk about the tragedies they experienced in Laos," said one college student active in the school for five years, since the beginning of her high school experience. The Jane Addams School "was an opportunity not only to help create something but also learn about myself, who I am and where I came from. It's been very interesting to listen to the women and to hear the stories. I needed to take time to learn about my Hmongness . . . where I came from, what my language is like, what my people have been through. It's been a journey of self-discovery. It has given me confidence to know at that place we can all be equal."[13]

For older immigrants, the Jane Addams School meets practical and pressing needs — studying for and passing the citizenship test to become a naturalized citizen; learning English; making personal connections with native-born U.S. citizens. It also serves for many as a schooling in American public life. When the school first opened, I was often struck by how many older Hmong women voiced the desire to learn how to act in public in the United States. "My life has changed [because of coming here]," a middle-aged woman told one evaluator. "I can communicate, understand English, and talk with whites." "I am becoming an important person to the rest of the community, going to Jane Addams," said another.[14]

The Jane Addams School developed many ways to combine grassroots organizing with appreciation for the learning resources of diverse ethnic and immigrant cultures. Each year since 1998, for instance, a summer Freedom Festival involves hundreds of new immigrants and neighborhood residents in a celebration of freedom, citizenship, and cultural practices. The Freedom Festival features bright Hmong dresses and Hmong dancing, colored kanga cloths from East Africa, and Latino designs—traditional Mexican attire, Guatemalan fabrics, and Andean wool—in a fashion show. Smells and sounds of Africa, Asia, and Latin America fill the air. Newly naturalized citizens are honored. In the summer of 2004, fifty-two were on stage. They told stories of journeys from Somalia, Mexico, Thailand, or Laos. Each year, elected officials give short speeches, and people are recognized for diverse political activities, from lobbying elected officials to participating in neighborhood projects. Aleida Benitez, who helped organize the first Freedom Festival and was honored herself as a naturalized citizen in 2004, says that the festival "unites the community and also celebrates diverse cultures through crafts, dance, music, and a fashion show. It's a way of honoring everyday heroes."[15]

The Jane Addams School offers experiences and opportunities for public development that feed powerfully into the Neighborhood Learning Community mission. "Some of the people in this community were leaders in Laos, in Thailand, and in Latin America," says Nan Skelton. "But many have not been able to translate that leadership to the incredibly different world of the St. Paul school system." Skelton observes that most institutions, including schools, discourage people from displaying their cultures and languages. "They want people to be proficient in the dominant culture." But the philosophy of the Jane Addams School is that "communities cannot build a future if they don't bring their past with them. [Public] leadership training [is essential] to help community leaders interact with and influence that world." The expectation of the Jane Addams School approach is that increased parent power will increase the capacity of the schools to teach. "We expect teachers and administrators of neighborhood schools will also seek ways to increase shared ownership in children's learning."[16]

Other groups involved in the Neighborhood Learning Community bring organizing experiences and skills that create learning resources. The Youth Farm and Market Project was started in 1999 by Gunnar

Liden, a participant in Jane Addams School who negotiated with La Puerta Abierta, a local church, for the use of some of their vacant land. The Youth Farm works with neighborhood children and youth to grow food in community gardens and sell it at a local market. It also includes a strong focus on youth development and organizing skills. The West Side Citizens Organization was founded in 1973 as the West Side's permanent neighborhood organization, growing from a successful battle with the city to get a new building for Humboldt High School. It has continued as an activist organizing force in the neighborhood over the years.

These groups joined with Community Education, the Parks and Recreation Department, the West Side Family Center, and others to explore what a neighborhood-wide organizing effort to create a culture of learning might look like. Reflecting an open, evolving, citizen-designed approach, there were many discussions and interviews with diverse stakeholders in the community. Riverview Library housed an effort called the Community Information Corps, in which teenagers, coached by adults, interviewed neighborhood residents and surveyed hidden learning resources in the community. They also created a website to display the resources and let others know about them. To create a wider sense of community ownership, the Neighborhood Learning Community also developed an initiative of mini-grants, from $50 to $1,500, for learning projects led by young people and community residents and also for parents and community groups for school-related initiatives. Among the early recipients were elementary school students who created a tour of the West Side based on oral histories and a local artist who produced a photographic display at the local neighborhood market showing the cultural diversity of the area.

Over the years, a number of different initiatives have developed as part of the Neighborhood Learning Community.

YOUTH APPRENTICESHIP PROJECT The Youth Apprenticeship Project was first proposed by a group of teenagers in one of the public housing projects on the West Side who were working with children to create new learning activities. When adults in the Neighborhood Learning Community asked what the teenagers would like for themselves, all responded "paid jobs," but they also emphasized the desire for employment where they could contribute to the neighborhood, develop work skills, and learn about possible career paths after high school. In 2003 the Youth Apprenticeship Project began.

Each summer, approximately twenty-five teenagers spend ten weeks working in a West Side business or organization, under supervision of a mentor. They also meet each week for a three-hour leadership meeting conducted by adult coaches from the neighborhood. The meetings are designed to integrate work and its civic meanings. They also create opportunities for the apprentices to discuss challenges at their workplace, what they are learning, and to explore a unifying theme.

In 2005, apprentices created oral histories with a diverse group of West Side residents and created an exhibit at the Minnesota Children's Museum. Many describe new public skills and concepts they have learned. "When I first started, I was really shy," said Chao Moua, who helped plan the Freedom Festival as part of his summer work. "Now I see how things get planned, and I know I have the power to do what I want. I've learned that it's not easy to plan a community festival. I got to do public speaking, and I feel more comfortable talking in front of others now."[17]

ALL AROUND THE NEIGHBORHOOD All Around the Neighborhood (AATN) has brought together seventeen organizations on the West Side to offer learning camps for children ages six to twelve. Camps teach different topics, from science (when I visited in the summer of 2006, students explained to me what they were learning about the life cycles of butterflies, and one teen showed me her cocoon) to art and neighborhood history. A strong emphasis in AATN is to teach young people about the neighborhood itself as a treasure trove of learning possibilities, much of it through everyday and informal encounters.

One community teacher described what happened on a walk. "We came across an older man patching the sidewalk. He explained . . . why he was patching and how he prepared the concrete. Another experience . . . was talking with a Hispanic woman working in her garden." In the community teacher's view, "the experience of connecting with people made the community real to them." It also provided real-world experiences. "We walked by another yard that had a barking dog," she remembered. "One boy was deathly afraid, thinking the dog might eat him." But other kids explained that if they stayed away, the dog wouldn't hurt them, and dogs don't eat you. "Having the kids explain helped him deal with his fear, and this was an experience he never would have had in a classroom."[18] In 2005, AATN expanded to offer learning opportunities through the year.

One important feature of AATN is a free bus called the West Side Circulator, which travels a 7.5 mile loop around the neighborhood. The Circulator stops at learning sites and public places like the Boys & Girls Club, Our Lady of Guadalupe church, and Torre de San Miguel public housing. "The Circulator is a visible symbol that shows . . . how learning happens in many places, not just the school," says Nan Kari, one of the organizers of the Neighborhood Learning Community. More than 6,300 riders used the Circulator in the first summer, 2003. Bus drivers learned children's names; parents often went along for the ride. "The Circulator is the kind of thing that might not show up on people's radar screen in terms of learning because it's not formal learning," said Bob Cudahy, a school teacher himself. "But it makes educational opportunities possible. It's important to get kids to programs, keeping them thinking, and helping them become lifelong learners."[19]

EDUCATORS INSTITUTE Another area of emphasis has been creating bridges between the neighborhood and area schools. In the summer of 2005, after tension with a local school about use of buildings for a computer project, Neighborhood Learning Community leaders organized a work group with the St. Paul school system to explore strategies for improving the relationship between schools and neighborhoods across the city. In 2006 a formal partnership was developed between Cherokee Heights Elementary School and AATN. And since 2003, the Neighborhood Learning Community has sponsored an Educators Institute (originally a teachers institute that was broadened to include educators as well). The Educators Institute offered credit-bearing classes designed to connect the school curriculum to the neighborhood and to develop team-oriented projects. Participants developed a collective vision: "People of all ages are supported by formal and informal learning experiences where everyone is a teacher, a learner, and a member of the community."

CIVIC POLICY From the outset, the Neighborhood Learning Community's vision of culture change has aimed at renewing Minnesota traditions that tie education to the civic life of communities. Thus, it developed relationships with a diversity of policymakers, including school board members, city council members, staff of various city departments, and the mayor elected in 2005, Chris Coleman. In May 2006, the Neighborhood Learning Community published *A Community Alive with Learning*, its five-year report, and sponsored a conference well attended by neighborhood leaders, school board members, city staff, and Coleman, who had made the idea of expanded community-based learning opportunities a major theme in his election campaign. Coleman picked up the theme of culture change, the shift from me to we. He also declared that the Neighborhood Learning Community would be a key model for an initiative called the Second Shift. Coleman and his staff, working with leaders of the Neighborhood Learning Community, have developed a vision of St. Paul as a state and national model of a whole city taking responsibility for its children's learning.

In the 2007 legislative session, the city—with help from Nora Slawik, a founder of the Citizen Legislators—successfully pressed for resources to expand the Neighborhood Learning Community circulator bus in several other neighborhoods. A number of Minnesota foundations joined in. By the summer, the new circulator buses were proving to be tools for neighborhood-wide organizing. And the learning outcomes were vivid. Jeannette Behr, research manager for the League of Minnesota Cities, observed that the community learning initiatives in St. Paul were "certainly more elaborate and more detailed than anything I've heard of." Meanwhile, young people themselves—many of whom helped lobby legislators for circulator bus support—voiced their own testimony. Ally Ojekwe, an eleven year old, took the circulator on the West Side to go to the Smart Girls summer group at the Boys & Girls Club. "We're learning about new things," she explained with a grin.[20]

The cooperation between the Neighborhood Learning Community and city leadership suggests possibilities for citizen involvement as agents and architects of culture change, along with a view of civil servants as more organizers than bureaucrats, information providers, or service deliverers. And it involves a different understanding of a professional—shifting from the outside expert to the fellow citizen.

Eighth Civic Skill: Getting to Know Your Neighborhood

Every neighborhood is unique. And getting to know the history, cultures, interests, power dynamics, and institutions of your neighborhood is a foundation for effective action. A neighborhood involves many dimensions: cultures and ethnic groups, institutions and places of employment (governmental, business, civic), stories, symbols, public spaces, interesting characters. Every neighborhood also has things that make it unique, and understanding these can generate multiple resources for action. Think in terms of how the issue or project you want to address can be furthered by tying it to the neighborhood.

TIPS AND TOOLS[21]

Map the neighborhood: Think about features of your community: distinctive features that make your community unique or different; people others look to for stories, knowledge, and wisdom; religious groups, public agencies, voluntary and hobby groups; historical sites; businesses.

Resources for action: What are the visible or buried resources in your neighborhood that might be engaged for action on your issue or project?

9 Citizen Professionals

Citizen professionals need to shift from acting as outside experts who fix problems to working collaboratively with their fellow citizens. This shift depends on professionals developing civic identities once again — and seeing themselves "on tap, not on top." The civic efforts of professionals show the importance of having wisdom, not simply knowledge.

DESPITE THE WAYS IN WHICH OUR WORLD IS TECHNOCRATIC, with experts in charge, broad forces are also at work to democratize knowledge. While large institutions try mightily to keep secrets, they find it harder and harder to do so. One of the distinctive features of the knowledge revolution today is that information is harder and harder to hoard (community organizing lore abounds with stories of the inside sympathizer who leaks information at critical moments of a community struggle against a bank or developer or chemical company). Information is not used up if it is given out. In many cases, it increases in value. Efforts to hoard information can lead to stagnation — a lesson learned by Soviet bloc officials, by tobacco company executives, and by intelligence officials after September 11. Information lends itself to sharing transactions.

If it is unusual to think about the values and concepts that frame and guide activity in this time of excessive specialization, skillful efforts to do so produce considerable power. Anne Fadiman, describing the disastrous encounter between American medical practice and Hmong culture in her book *The Spirit Catches You and You Fall Down,* also recounts striking examples of alternative democratic practice that increased the power and effectiveness of professionals who showed respect and paid attention. Doctors like Dwight Conquergood were successful in introducing public health practices in Thai refugee camps by drawing on Hmong cultural symbols and by showing connections between western medicine and traditional practices. The power dynamics in this process — a productive conception of power, rather than simply a view of power as static, zero-sum force — are analyzed in more detail in the Afterword.

The explosion of the Internet in recent years — the World Wide Web, blogs, Internet journalism, and a host of other innovations — has begun to create a new context for professionals. One way to describe the professionals who decide to work *with* citizens, rather than acting *on* them, is that they are "citizen professionals." Citizen professionals are proud of their knowledge and the craft of their discipline, but they also know their limits. Citizen professionals are citizens who see their specialized knowledge as "on tap, not on top," in the words of community organizers. They recognize that solving complex problems requires many sources and kinds of knowledge. Minnesotans are pioneering in this approach.

The Making of Citizen Professionals

Civic life depends on professionals who see their work in communal and public terms. In recent decades professional development programs have taught professionals to look at people in terms of their deficiencies, not their assets, and to be detached from the civic life of communities. This view weakens professionals' own citizenship, creates standardized, uprooted models of professional practice, and erodes civic muscle. It also is a little-observed cause of subtle patterns of racial and class prejudice among professional elites. Today, professionals are trained to think in highly individualist terms, detached from civic and communal life.

In her study of professional graduate education, *Professional Identity Crisis*, Carrie Yang Costello finds that aspiring professionals from minority backgrounds often face a forced choice between their home cultural communities and professional cultures. This creates a serious "identity dissonance." As one Filipino student put it, "In the legal culture you have to adopt a different way of being, a different vocabulary and way to carry yourself. . . . When I go home, if I act the way I do [at Berkeley law school], my cousins and my friends say, 'You're kind of whitewashed.'"[1]

Citizen professionals develop unique styles grounded in local civic cultures. They learn respect for the insights of those without formal credentials. They recognize that they have much to learn from communities where populist values of cultural roots, community vitality, and equality are alive. They also build skills of collaborative public work that help energize and activate broad civic energies.

A recent collection by Scott Peters and his colleagues, *Engaging Campus and Community*, recounts stories of University of Minnesota scientists who have public-work practices. Scholars who engage in public work, whether in weed science or sustainable agriculture, develop relational and organizing skills that are not taught in graduate school. They gain respect for local knowledge and culture. They develop a sense of everyday politics as the negotiation of the gritty plurality of the human condition. They function in open-ended ways. They recognize their own uncertainties. And they move from critique to engagement, integrating their specialized knowledge into a larger project. As a result, such citizen scientists help to create wisdom in the communities in which they work, bringing knowledge of larger contexts, catalyzing reflection on the values and civic meanings buried in even the most seemingly mundane of topics, such as weed control. Two examples from Minnesota illustrate such principles.

Laurie McGinnis

Laurie McGinnis, associate director of the Center for Transportation Studies at the University of Minnesota and one of the state's most respected civil engineers, describes her dawning recognition of what her formal education lacked. She earned a bachelor of science degree in civil and environmental engineering at the University of Wisconsin, with a concentration on structures. In her view, her education "provided me with a well-developed skill set for analyzing a structural frame, designing a steel bridge beam, and performing a cost-benefit analysis." But it had limits. "The curriculum was devoid of any content that addressed the public affairs element of the civil engineering profession. There wasn't a single mention of the concept of place or of the significant relationship between the profession of civil engineering and creating place. I had no opportunities to take courses that exposed me to the political aspects of enhancing a community through engineering projects or equipped me with public engagement skills to accomplish this goal."[2]

Several years into her professional career McGinnis gained valuable, firsthand experience with the political aspects of transportation projects, the skills of engagement, and the importance of place. "I had the incredible good fortune to be on the design team for two of the Twin Cities' premier river crossings — first the Hennepin Avenue suspension bridge and then the Lake Street-Marshall Avenue arch bridge. The primary lesson learned on the Hennepin Avenue project was that the era of 'the professional knows best' was over." Local citizens had organized in opposition to the proposed bridge, which in their view did not fit the history of the neighborhood. Hennepin Avenue was the location of the first bridge crossing the Mississippi River in Minneapolis. Citizens and local business people thought that the replacement bridge should mimic the original design. Lawsuits and protests ensued. "This experience clearly marked a turning point in my development as a transportation professional. I was able to see that the process of creating public-works projects would be changing, but I was not able to predict to what extent that process would change or how I needed to prepare myself to adapt to that change."

Several years later, McGinnis was design engineer on the Lake Street–Marshall Avenue replacement bridge. Again, a group of local citizens had organized in opposition, believing that the proposed bridge was not consistent with the history of the area, nor did it connect with the most significant marker of the place — the Mississippi River Parkway. "This time, the group of citizens was successful in developing a public relationship with leaders at the Minnesota Department of Transportation before a lawsuit was initiated." Mn/DOT convened a committee of residents, business owners, technical experts (her consultant firm), and members of the agency to oversee selection and design of the aesthetic elements of the bridge, with the goal of integrating the new structure with the surrounding environment and the historical context of the area. Mn/DOT recognized that the committee was a vehicle for coordinating actions, building mutual understanding and trust, and fostering problem solving. "Ultimately, the committee was successful in choosing and recommending the set of aesthetic treatments that are present on and around the bridge today," McGinnis concluded. "The entire community has a public place for which they feel ownership and pride."

McGinnis sees the transportation professional evolving into a citizen professional as the future of the profession. The Minnesota Department of Transportation is a national leader in the implementation of an approach that seeks to integrate transportation projects into community values. The approach has six key principles:

· Balance safety, mobility, community, and environmental goals in all projects.

· Involve the public and affected agencies early and continuously.

· Use an interdisciplinary team tailored to project needs.

· Address all modes of travel.

· Apply flexibility inherent in design standards.

· Incorporate aesthetics as an integral part of good design.

McGinnis sees much more ahead. "Transportation has the potential to be a community-builder in ways similar to the best public buildings. To use transportation as a community-builder, community members must be fully engaged in conceiving and creating the work, so they feel ownership of the outcome. Rather than arriving with a preconceived plan, professionals must actively work with the community as citizens who possess one set of knowledge and skills engaged with citizens who possess other important knowledge and skills. A citizen professional can bring a disciplined process to the group, but it is very important for the professional to serve in the role of resource rather than expert and to maintain a minimally hierarchical structure within the group."

McGinnis's understanding of the citizen transportation professional draws in significant ways on the work of William (Bill) Doherty who is a pioneer in this innovative and important field.

Bill Doherty

William Doherty, professor of family social science at the University of Minnesota, is a past president of the National Council of Family Practice. He has built Families and Democracy, a group of partnerships based on a public and civic approach to professional work in the family-oriented professions. Doherty described at length the changes this involved.[3]

In 1985, I had my progressive critique of materialism and consumerism in American culture well in place. I saw my world, the therapists' world, as the good guys. We were on the side of the angels. But I must have been open to some self-reflection. When I saw the review of *Habits of the Heart* by Robert Bellah and colleagues in 1985, something told me it would be good for me to read it. I got the book to expand my critique of what was going on in American society, not to be challenged in my own work.

In one of the early chapters, the authors asked a therapist in California why she was committed to her children. She answered exactly the way I would have answered: "These are my values. I would feel guilty if I abandoned my children." The interviewers probed more deeply. "Would she want others to hold similar values?" She said, "Everyone has to choose their own values. It's not for me to impose values on others."

My hair stood up as I read this passage. I sat in the chair transfixed. It was shocking that this therapist could not speak in terms of public morality. Tomorrow she could wake up with a revised set of values. The authors were not saying she's an immoral person. They acknowledged that she probably was as committed to her children as any of us. I don't know that I would have been any more articulate about my own values as a parent if they had asked me. But I realized that I had bought into the discourse of private psychology. I was never the same. I realized that my profession and I were part of the problem, not just part of the solution to our country's social problems.

I recently heard a presentation by four senior family therapy scholars who were regretting that they had not made more of their careers, having been buried in day-to-day teaching and clinical administration and worrying that their research had not made a difference for practitioners. I was sitting in the same room feeling fired up about my work, partly because I see myself as a catalyst and not as a lone ranger. Some of the difference is inborn temperament (I got the optimistic Irish genes, not the depressive ones), but some of it is working with a different paradigm. Citizenship work has transformed my career and renewed the sense of idealism that brought me to this field.

I began to read about public work—professional practice that is politically energizing, catalytic, civically educative, and politically effective. It helped me develop a conceptual framework for action as a therapist. I had been giving talks to a variety of community groups about strengthening family life. The action breakthrough was in Wayzata, Minnesota, in April 1998. I talked with a large group of parents at a parent fair. The parents were lit up over the problem of feeling out of control of their time but afraid to get off the treadmill. A middle school principal said, "We're part of this problem. We offer so many activities to kids that if parents agree to half of them, they're not going to have much of a family life left."

That was the dawning for me that this issue of over-scheduling was not just an individual family issue, but also a cultural issue. It was a structural issue as well. I talked to other people. Light bulbs started coming on for them and me both. Family time is a public issue.

A couple of months later, the organizer of the original parent fair asked me to come back next year and give that talk again. That was the moment that I decided to go for it. I turned her down. "I don't want to give Doherty's greatest hits. But if you want to take on this problem as a community, I've been learning a model to do this, and I'd be willing to come back and work with you to figure out how to do it." We organized a town meeting for the following spring.

About seventy people, including parents, school board people, and community leaders, came. These people were ready. I began by asking, "Are these things we are talking about here — over-scheduled kids and under-connected families — only individual family problems or are they also community problems? Are the solutions only individual family solutions, or are they also community solutions? What can we do about the problems as a community?"

It was an electrifying experience. When it was over, participants had decided to do something about the problem and, among other things, formed a community activation team. That group ultimately became the steering group for Putting Family First.

Putting Family First helped stimulate the national movement and debate about family over-scheduling and consumer pressures. It was the inspiration for groups like Balance4Success in the southern suburbs of the Twin Cities. It also began the creation of the Families and Democracy partnerships in which Doherty, a group of his graduate students and colleagues, and citizen leaders have come to see themselves as cultural organizers to transform the me-first culture. "The me-first culture cuts across the parenting issues, the marriage questions, the anxiety of parents about whether they can make it, the isolation of couples," says Doherty. "It's something bigger—there's a cultural crisis." Doherty has come to focus on what he calls pressure points, "where people feel the pinch, and where they can make a connection between the personal and the public."[4]

This is a different approach than the expert model he learned in his professional training. For instance, Doherty's partnership with the Minnesota Early Childhood Family Education network called Community Engaged Parent Education, or CEPE, grows from the knowledge of parent educators themselves.

Early Childhood Family Education (ECFE) is the largest early childhood and parent education program in the nation. ECFE is offered in almost every Minnesota school district and involves about 250,000 families with children under five each year. It has a history of collaborative learning approaches that involve parents through parent education groups. In ECFE, licensed parent educators meet weekly for a school year with groups of about fifteen parents. These meetings over an extended period provide ECFE educators with many opportunities to build relationships with parents.

In 1999, Doherty approached several ECFE programs with the idea of expanding the reach of traditional parent education to include a civic engagement dimension. With the co-leadership of Beth Cutting, a St. Paul ECFE teacher who pioneered this way of working in her own teaching, he has partnered with senior parent educators in three school districts to develop Community Engaged Parent Education. Since that time, with support from the McKnight Foundation, the Community Engaged Parent Education effort has developed a group of thirty-one parent educators who have created many ways to raise the public side of parenting questions such as how to deal with aggressive behavior.

The mission of Community Engaged Parent Education is to develop the capacity of parents for citizen deliberation and action on public issues related to children's well being. "The key principle of CEPE is that all personal parenting concerns, without exception, have public dimensions," says Doherty. "This means that community issues are not add-ons in parent education; they are part of the core, along with traditional issues such as child development and discipline. The key skills are to weave the public dimensions of parenting seamlessly into the discussion of personal parenting concerns, and to facilitate personal and collective action on issues that are of concern to parents. What emerges is a civic consciousness in parents and a readiness, when the issue and time are right, to take a variety of action steps."[5]

In dozens of communities, parent education classes have become sites and seedbeds for civic discussion and places from which civic action can grow. Evaluations for the McKnight Foundation in 2006 showed deliberation on more than seventy-five public topics. Parents discussed many questions, including lack of family time and over-scheduled kids, sex education, media influences, neighborhood safety, and many others. And parents reported organizing civic action on issues such as school lunches, immigration, school nutrition, and addressing hyper-consumerist birthday parties.

A key to the growth of Community Engaged Parent Education was the realization that publicly oriented family educators like Beth Cutting were doing public work. A good deal of the task of spreading this public craft was helping her identify and name what she was doing. Then, she and other parent educators and parents developed skills in mentoring others.

Drawing on the practical wisdom of others, whether professionals or amateurs, has informed other partnership projects. Families Formation is an initiative in which young African American parents who are interested in developing stable relationships and families learn from "the real experts"—those like themselves who have succeeded without any formal credentials. Other programs have identified models and sources of inspiration for projects such as the Extended Family Network, a movement among African American families in the Twin Cities based on what Eric Yancey, one of the cofounders, called "intentionality." In the Extended Family Network, clusters of families set monthly goals and hold each other accountable. They also make a collective commitment to be involved in the significant moments of a child's life. "When my brother was playing football, he would have four 'uncles' out there. It's mushroomed," said Yancey. Fifty-five families were in the network by 2006.[6]

Birthdays Without Pressure

On January 14, 2007, a new partnership project, Birthdays Without Pressure, was publicly launched, following a year of one-on-one interviews, strategy sessions, meetings, and planning done by a group of parents. Bill Doherty and the other organizers see it as another front of "cultural organizing to shift from me-first to we." One of the features of this effort, like many of Doherty's projects, is that the parents did almost all the work—he calculated that he had only spent about forty-eight hours on the project over the year.

Children's birthdays may seem innocuous. But the group collected a growing number of horror stories, including a four-year-old girl mauled by a cougar providing birthday party entertainment; seven year olds picked up in stretch limos to attend a classmate's birthday party; and a one-year-old's party that featured gift openings lasting two hours.[7]

Michelle West had had enough after she created a ballerina theme for her daughter's sixth birthday party and spent hours driving around town just to find the perfect figurines to decorate the cake. Then her daughter refused to taste it.

West joined with a group of parents who worked with Doherty on the birthday party issue. They tried out frameworks that would be non-judgmental. "Instead of finger wagging about consumer culture, we wanted to stress that we all face enormous cultural pressures to keep up with the Joneses," said Doherty. "We need to band together to turn this around."

The launch produced an amazing outpouring of energy. Six hundred news stories were published across the country and around the world within ten days. Doherty participated in more than sixty interviews, while the group did many more. They had over twenty thousand visits a day to the group's website (www.birthdayswithoutpressure.org). And reporters and journalists recounted their own experiences.

"When our middle daughter was three, she had her first big birthday party, a cookout with our neighbors and their kids," said Sam Barnes, an editor at the *Minneapolis Star Tribune.* "Laura sat regally at the head of the picnic table, holding court. When the guests began to leave, I reached for her plate and said, 'Sweetie, the party's over.' Satisfaction

TABLE 3

WHO IS THE PROFESSIONAL?

	Outside Expert	Citizen Professional
Motive	Altruistic service	Co-creation and joint problem solving
Who is in charge?	Experts	Citizens, both professionals and amateurs
Goal	To fix problems	To solve problems while also building community ties
Method	Expert intervention	Public work
Approach to teaching	Expository, didactic	Apprenticeship, relational, conveying craft heritage
Sources of knowledge	Abstract theory, book learning	Local situation, experience, and practice as well as theory
Skills	Disaggregation, analysis, application	Synthesis, integration, contextual understanding, relationship building
Key role of professionals	Service provider	Catalyst

gave way to utter despair. 'But I don't want the party to be over,' she said, again and again."

I asked Doherty what was going on with this kind of response. "Almost everyone — certainly all the organizing group of parents — sees runaway birthday parties as simply an example of a much bigger problem, the hypercompetitive, individualistic consumer culture — the runaway me-first culture. But it's too big to get a handle on, and most who try take a judgmental approach. What Birthdays Without Pressure does is show one way to take action. It has generated an explosion of hope."

Underlying all the Families and Democracy partnerships is the potential in the immense untapped talent, energy, and knowledge of families and citizens. This philosophy is expressed in a new effort to create a citizen professional center at the University of Minnesota's College of Education. It will draw on Doherty's partnerships, the Center for Democracy and Citizenship, and a project at the Academic Health Center called the Citizen Health Care Program, which joins together several colleagues including Doherty, his student Tai Mendenhall, and his colleague Macaran Baird, chair of the department of family medicine.

Citizen professionalism points toward a fundamentally different civic philosophy than the outside-expert philosophy that now dominates in Minnesota and other places. It suggests a philosophy of shared abundance, of common wealth, not scarcity. This has implications for many professional systems and practices today, across different fields. It also has implications for the renewal of government of the people and by the people, not only for the people.

Ninth Civic Skill: Developing a Citizen Identity

The old saw says, "If you think of yourself as a hammer, then everything looks like a nail." Today, people are usually educated to look at the world in terms of their specific profession or discipline — health, law, teaching, engineering, internet technology. The key to effective action is to put your own "hammer" in relation to many other ways of looking at the world—what can be called "citizen professionalism," people working collaboratively with others to solve public problems and create common things. When we did interviews with many civil servants during the New Citizenship project with the White House, the most striking finding was that beyond any specific methods and tools, highly successful people said, in the words of Jerome Delli Priscoli, "The crucial thing is to put the 'civil' back in civil service," learning to think of themselves first and foremost as citizens working with other citizens.

A basic civic skill is to learn to think and act as a citizen, working with others in collaborative ways on the basis of appreciation for the talents and intelligence of everyone, whether they are in your field or not. This takes time and learning.

TIPS AND TOOLS

History: Learning about and publicizing traditions and examples of citizen professionals in your neighborhood or community is often a first step. Who were the civic leaders of your area who worked to build the civic and public life of the community?

Who are you? Why did you go into the line of work or volunteer commitment that you did? Did it have strong public components? What have you learned about working on an equal, collaborative basis with others through your work? What obstacles have emerged?

Role models: Do a one-on-one interview with someone you respect as a citizen professional—someone working in any field (teaching, medicine, business, government work, etc.) who has a commitment to the community and is able to work with others outside their field on the basis of respect and partnership.

House meetings: Hold a house meeting with a group of professionals—your own profession or occupation, if possible—about why they got involved in their work in the first place. Did they have public motivations? What have been their experiences with trying to act on them?

Professional allies: What professionals are on your interest and power maps that you might enlist? Do a one-on-one to find out their interests.

10 Renewing Government of the People

Political leaders and civil servants seeking to strengthen civic life help return us to a government of the people, by the people, for the people. Citizens outside of government who remember that the government is *us*, not them, claim the station of citizenship. They shift from being childlike protestors or dependents to being adult partners. Both sides help create the shift from scarcity to abundance.

F OR ALL IT MIGHT SEEM THAT THE WAR BETWEEN LIBERALS and conservatives is entrenched in Minnesota and elsewhere with no resolution in sight, I believe a *Star Tribune* editorial of 2005 headlined "Minnesota Shows Signs of Civic Revival" had it right. The paper's editors pointed to a civic stirring that is profoundly important. This is much more than increasing the number of volunteers or expanding the number of voters in elections. A civic revival can change our public conversation, widen our horizons, and shift us from a politics of scarcity to a politics of abundance.[1]

One necessary change involves rethinking the role of government and other institutions, now mainly service providers but potentially, as they once were, catalysts. Catalytic government helps to generate abundance by multiplying the civic energies and talents available to solve problems, produce commonwealth, and build communities. Below the surface, strong examples of catalytic government have appeared.

The Commonwealth of Burnsville

In 1994, after serving on the Burnsville city council, Elizabeth Kautz campaigned for mayor of the southern Minneapolis suburb on the slogan, "Government doesn't have to be bad!" She wanted a return to a view of government as a catalyst for generating civic energy and engagement, not mainly as a service provider. "All of us together need to create a citizenry that is empowered to do the work of the public," she said. "Government can help. But in an era of limited resources and great challenges, I can't pretend that government alone can fix it anymore, and, besides, coming together to solve problems engages the people of the community and everyone will experience a sense of purpose, involvement, success, and pride."[2]

When teenage skateboarders got in trouble with the law for skating in school parking lots, Kautz asked them what could be done to change their behavior. "If you get us a skateboard park, we'll stop skating where we're not supposed to," they said. Kautz replied, "I agree you need a place to enjoy your sport, but we are not going to build the park for you. However, I will work with you and together we can build a park for you to enjoy and practice your sport. What I will do is bring people together and I can open some doors. But you're going to have to organize all of the kids and the parents." Working with several adults, the teenagers negotiated agreements with service clubs, businesses, and insurance companies. They raised money, developed a design, and gained support from the city to build the park. The city identified land within the Civic Center for the park, and city employees, along with volunteers from the businesses and service organizations, helped build it.

The skateboard story is part of a wider effort at civic renewal in Burnsville called Partnerships for Tomorrow. The overall objective has been to rebuild the civic life of Burnsville by tapping latent human talents and other resources in new ways. Kautz described Burnsville as a "commonwealth" and "a community of abundance." Government work was redesigned and clustered in six priority areas set by citizens: safety, youth, neighborhoods, development and redevelopment, environment, and transportation. The mayor and council added Financial Management and Service Delivery to those priorities identified by the citizens. The city and residents formed substantial partnerships in each area.

The Burnsville initiative hinged on a fundamental redefinition of government's role. "We've had to get beyond customer service, so that public outcomes are widely owned by the citizens," explained Kautz. City manager Greg Konat pointed out that this is difficult, given dominant assumptions on both sides. Civil servants are trained to think of citizens as clients and, more recently, as customers. "Moving beyond the customer service model has meant that we had to recognize that we can't do all the public tasks in government, even if we'd like to. Rather than just provide services, we redefined our overall objectives as helping to build community."[3]

This meant a change in identity for city workers. It returns "civil" to "civil service," with city employees coming to see themselves as citizen professionals working with other citizens. "This shift in identity is not easy for a lot of people in government, but it's critical," Konat said. While city government continued to emphasize "quality service," government workers shifted their focus away from seeing citizens as customers. "Now we serve more as the catalyst," explained Konat. "We help call meetings together in the neighborhoods or with business or with schools. Government has a role. We can provide certain expertise. But most of the answers have to come from within the community."

This sort of approach has begun to spread, under the surface of the dominant paradigm. Frank Benest, based on his experiences as city manager in Palo Alto, California, contrasts catalytic local government of the sort practiced in Burnsville—government as barn-raising—with the model of government as a vending machine, based on customer service. In the vending-machine model, the dominant approach, citizens put in their money in the form of taxes and scream and yell if they don't get what they want.[4] He suggests four strategies for a catalytic, barn-raising approach, all of which can be found in Burnsville:

· Government needs to bring together diverse interests to envision a future.

· Government needs to join with others in developing community leadership.

· Government needs to work through mediating institutions such as civic groups and religious organizations.

· Government needs to have a strong focus on empowering neighborhoods to take action on common concerns.

Reviving the Legacy of Public Work

Since the outset of the work at the Humphrey Institute's Center for Democracy and Citizenship, we have sought to advance the concept of government of the people and by the people, a catalyst for the public work of citizens and civic institutions. This meant finding stories like those from Burnsville. It also meant recalling traditions that had been largely forgotten.

In conventional historical treatments, the Progressive movement of the first decades of the twentieth century is often defined simply in terms of the ideas of its centralizing advocates like Walter Lippmann and Herbert Croly, who were full of faith in science and the wisdom of technocrats.[5]

Yet we discovered a more democratic underside of Progressive history, in which government interacted in fluid, generative ways with an array of civic groups. Jane Addams, founder of Hull House, exemplified this perspective. She was an insightful critic of the detachment of professionals and government from the experience and everyday lives of ordinary people. She argued that teachers, for instance, needed to see their roles in catalytic terms; the purpose of education was not mainly instruction but rather "to free the powers of each man and connect him with the rest of life," the larger democracy. Professional practice of any sort needed to release and develop the productive energies and powers of people.[6]

Viewpoints like Jane Addams' were associated with the belief that government is a civic catalyst, not a substitute for citizen efforts or a service provider. The national Cooperative Extension System was an important outgrowth of this view. Indeed, architects of the Cooperative Extension System saw themselves creating "rural settlements" of the sort Addams had founded in Hull House, or like Phyllis Wheatley in the Twin Cities. They sought to develop an understanding of public agencies that took account of the dramatic advances of science, communications, technology, and other developments in the twentieth century and integrated them into a vision of a vital rural civic life sustained by the people themselves.

In *Engaging Campus and Community*, Scott Peters writes about Liberty Hyde Bailey, dean of agriculture at Cornell, who was chair of Theodore Roosevelt's Country Life Commission, which outlined the Extension philosophy. Bailey was a champion of this approach. "Students in agriculture are doing much more than fitting themselves to follow an occupation," he wrote. "They are to take part in a great regeneration. The student in agriculture is fitting himself for a great work." Bailey challenged technocratic approaches to Extension work. "A prevailing idea seems to be that an expert shall go into the community and give advice to the farmers on the running of their farms and on all sorts of agricultural subjects," he said. This approach did little good, in his view. Even when it conveyed information, it created dependencies, not capacities for cooperative action. "The redirection of any civilization must rest primarily on the people who comprise it, rather than be imposed from persons in other conditions of life."[7]

In his view, rural communities faced many tangible problems. But the most important problem was a crisis in confidence and morale, a sense of victimhood fed by the condescending views of urban elites. "Our present greatest need is the development of what might be called 'the community sense,' the idea of the community as a whole working together toward one work," he wrote.[8]

This required revitalization of every rural institution, from churches and women's clubs to business groups, from cooperative creameries to local political parties. Above all, institutions like schools and churches needed to come alive with community spirit. They needed to engage their members in the problems of life, have stronger connections to rural history and values, and be governed by rural people themselves instead of distant state bureaucrats. His belief that education needed to connect students with the life of communities, and that schools should be social centers for community life, fed into the Minnesota tradition of education. "We must outgrow the sit-still and keep-still method of school work," he declared. "I want to see our country school-houses without screwed down seats, and to see the children put to work with tools and soils and plants and problems."[9] Bailey's views shaped the Cooperative Extension System, embodied in the idea that its most basic task was not dissemination of information but rather organizing work that developed rural communities' capacities for cooperative self-action.

Cooperative Extension, funded through a mix of federal, state, and county dollars and tied to land-grant universities like the University of Minnesota, had lost some of its civic dimensions in the state and elsewhere as its mission had shifted to technology transfer. But top state leaders proved responsive to reinvigorating the catalytic roles of Extension agents, seeing agents as organizers who helped communities to define their own problems and develop solutions. "We're going back to the way Extension started, with citizenship and public work," explained Pat Borich, who led several years of change that involved reinventing Extension in civic terms. This meant system-wide reform, including new, decentralized patterns of decision making, staff development at annual conferences, and protocols for staff performance review that were more interactive and designed to tap staff interests.[10]

A process of organizing training led by Carol Shields and Peg Michels shaped Extension practices in the state. "The introduction of the concept of 'public' gave people something larger than the immediate situation," said Shields, director of Minnesota 4-H. Shields said these ideas created space for reflective people to come to the forefront in a new way in the system. "There were some very good thinkers in the system, but it had not been a trait much valued. Talking about concepts like public work and citizenship created a different atmosphere where ideas could come to life."[11]

Minnesota had considerable influence for a time on other state Extension systems through its emerging civic practices. After coming to a training session organized by the University of Minnesota Extension service, Barbara Mobley returned to her home in Anniston, Alabama, to try something different. Mobley had been a Cooperative Extension county agent for twenty-nine years and had adopted the common information-dissemination and service-delivery approach. But she shifted to helping people organize their own problem-solving groups. This was not easy. "It means letting go of previous methods we used in prescribing a 'fix' for a community problem," she said. "We shared the ownership, and redefined our role to be a catalyst."[12]

As a result, many people began using Extension resources in new ways. An area-wide health council brought together public-health nurses, low-income mothers, and teenagers to tackle issues like teen pregnancy. A group called the Women's Empowerment Network provided training in everyday political skills and public speaking for low-income women. In another important example of action on a tough public problem, Cooperative Extension brought together a mix of community people and military personnel to develop a strategic plan for decommissioning chemical weapons. "On an issue like this, the military typically will say, 'If anything happens we'll let you know what to do,'" said Bill Salzer, an Auburn University professor knowledgeable about conflict resolution approaches. "This is ripe for panic. But Extension brought all the sides together."[13]

In the process, citizens developed skills in forming new public relationships; they learned about the complexity of the problem; and they generated many new resources. Extension offices became catalytic, generating a new sense of possibility and abundance. The southern region of Cooperative Extension subsequently sponsored a number of experiments in this approach across the South. The Kettering Foundation convened a group of state Extension leaders in Columbus, Ohio, to build on this history.

In 1993 and 1994, while working with the White House Domestic Policy Council, we drew on such experiences and others in the bipartisan New Citizenship effort coordinated by the Center for Democracy and Citizenship. Pat Borich presented the story of Minnesota Extension innovations in a high-level meeting of administration officials in the Roosevelt Room of the White House on Martin Luther King Day, January 14, 1994. A number of other meetings ensued. Many other civic and political leaders and institutions were involved. The group explored the concept of government as a catalytic resource for citizens, individually and collectively. In this perspective, government is not "the problem," as the conservative president Ronald Reagan was famously prone to describe it, but neither was it "the solution," as his liberal opponents were likely to argue. The centerpiece of the work with the White House was the proposition that policies and practices can be assessed by their positive or negative impact on citizenship and civic

capacity and that government needs to be held accountable for its overall civic impact.

Examining policies and practices through the lens of their impact on
civic life sheds new light on fields of youth development and education,
the environment, health, housing and urban development, higher education, and government reorganization and training practices. The
New Citizenship conducted hundreds of interviews in different federal
agencies, produced a number of working papers, and created the basis
for a day-long Camp David seminar on the future of citizenship with
President Bill Clinton and top administration officials in 1995.[14]

Over the years many federal agencies have made a shift from simple
service delivery to seeing government as a partner and catalyst. This
civic legacy has continued and evolved, under the surface of partisan
storms and acrimony, into the twenty-first century. Carmen Sirianni,
research director for the New Citizenship and professor of sociology at
Brandeis, writes in his forthcoming *Investing in Democracy*, "The Environmental Protection Agency has made critical contributions to catalyzing learning among extensive networks [such as] watershed groups,
schools and universities, scientists, and regulators. . . . [The agency] has
developed critical design components—funding, training, network
catalyst, technical assistance, data systems, management models, regu-
latory alignment—that make it increasingly possible for citizens to step
up to the plate, not just as advocates and protesters but as skilled and
effective co-producers of public goods and usable knowledge."[15]

The New Citizenship project also showed how much such ideas and
innovations go against the grain and how difficult it is to sustain them at
the highest levels of national politics. The Beltway leadership of Washington almost universally panned Clinton's 1995 State of the Union
message about the work of citizenship as naïve, unrealistic, and too self-
critical of the Beltway. Clinton quickly retreated. In states across the
country Cooperative Extension services battled to sustain civic pur-

poses in the face of expert-knowledge cultures. Many of the civic innovations that Borich and others championed eroded after his retirement in 1995.

Our experiences working with local governments, Minnesota Cooperative Extension, the New Citizenship, and other partnerships with the public sector taught us a key lesson for the emerging civic life movement: while local, state, and national leaders may find civic life ideas inspiring and have key roles to play in articulating them, a broad civic life movement with roots in many settings is necessary if we are to see the cultural change required for genuine social transformation.

At the same time, we also concluded that political leaders have distinctive leadership roles to play in moving from "me to we," articulating a new vision of civic life, and helping bring it about. Senator Dave Senjem, the Republican minority leader of the Minnesota state senate from Rochester, Minnesota, much concerned about unproductive partisan wrangling, argued, "Legislators have both a unique and significant opportunity to guide civic life."[16]

Political leaders can be contributors to citizenship and civic life in a variety of ways. Politicians can be civic philosophers, in the vein of Minnesota officeholders across both parties, including Hubert Humphrey, Walter Mondale, Elmer Andersen, Al Quie, Harry Davis, Paul Wellstone, Elizabeth Kautz, Elona Street-Stewart, Dave Senjem, Jim Scheibel, and Toni Carter. Politicians can be civic conveners of groups in their communities, bringing people together to discuss and work on issues across partisan and other divides. Political leaders can be civic architects of policies that catalyze public work and civic learning in communities, not simply deliver the goods. To help strengthen civic life across the state, we have sought to find such partners.

The New Civic Politics

Nora Slawik, Democratic representative from the suburban communities of Maplewood and Woodbury, ran for the state legislature after a history of frustrations dealing with bureaucracies for her son, who was in special education programs. She also felt government had become distant. "Politicians rank below used car salesmen in terms of popularity now. I wanted to bring government much closer to the people." Slawik became a leader in the Minnesota House of Representatives on the subject of early childhood issues, co-chairing the bicameral and bipartisan caucus on the topic. Then in the spring of 2006, as part of her midcareer master's degree program at the Humphrey Institute of Public Affairs, she took a course on organizing and public work taught by Dennis Donovan, national organizer of Public Achievement.

"It was called Organizing for Public Life. I have a public life and I need to be better organized, so I thought, maybe this will be beneficial," she laughed. She found the course themes provided ways to name things that politicians do instinctively but usually haven't thought about consciously. "For instance, we are used to small talk all the time, and then asking someone, 'What do you want?' But the one-on-one approach is different. It's really about getting to know someone."[17]

The distinction between a public life where one acts appropriately on principles like accountability and visibility and a private life where one looks for loyalty and nurturance helped to name many things Slawik felt were wrong with today's public arena. "It was like a light switch coming on." She also appreciated the stress on understanding self-interest, defined as the passions that move each individual and different from selflessness or selfishness. "It really challenges the partisan wrangling," Slawik believes. "Being able to be up front—I need this for my community, and you need that." The larger ideas of civic life and organizing also helped her experiment with concepts of hope, community, and abundance.

During the spring legislative session, Slawik asked her colleagues if they would be interested in discussions of civic trends in the state, as part of the house meeting series that Minnesota Works Together was organizing with many groups. The response was strong, despite the legislators' crowded schedules. Nineteen showed up at the first discussion and ten more at the second, a mix representing urban, suburban, and rural, both political parties, and both houses of the legislature. Dave Senjem agreed to help co-chair the discussions. He was part of a weekly community discussion in Rochester called Coffee and Conversation, convened each Saturday by a diverse group of political and civic leaders to discuss community issues—a great example of political leaders as conveners. Reflecting on his experiences, Senjem believes that partisan wrangling often means people lose focus. "Life's conflicts are only resolved through human interaction and agreement of contending parties," he says.

The house meetings at the legislature began with the question, "What are the civic life traditions that you value in your party?" It provoked surprising and often heated response. "I didn't run for office because of a political party!" said one state senator immediately. "I wanted to do things for my community. My frustration is how rarely this is the focus of what we talk about in the legislature." The discussion uncovered many other worries and discontents. One woman who had moved to the state from Arizona because of Minnesota's public spirit worried about the threat to the great tradition of civic life. Some expressed their concerns that many traditional gathering spaces where people meet across party lines are not widely used. "There is a dearth of intergenerational substantive talk," said one. Several said that consumerism is rampant. "We're working harder and harder to get 'more stuff.'"

Legislators had many ideas about what they could do to strengthen the civic roles of legislators. These included expanding programs like Public Achievement so young people could learn about everyday politics, convening citizens on these topics, developing a language of abundance, and looking at the civic roles that government can play. Many also expressed interest in creating a bipartisan, bicameral citizen legislator group to advance such ideas. Senjem and Slawik agreed to be co-chairs. In Senjem's view, "Working with the citizen legislator group provides a wonderful avenue for learning various styles and approaches to civic engagement and achieving community success." By the spring of 2007, the group was established.[18]

The New Civic Movement
James Madison wrote in 1788 that "No theoretical checks — no form of government — can render us secure. To suppose that any form of government will secure liberty or happiness without any virtue in the people is a chimerical idea."

Madison believed that popular government of any kind depended on active citizenship. This meant that citizens had to learn how to be citizens. At the times when Americans have become active contributors to our nation's commonwealth — such as the Great Depression and World War II — the government itself has become better. As the nation met the challenges of social ills like unemployment, bad housing, and poverty, ordinary people took center stage. President Franklin Roosevelt said, "Always the heart and soul of our country will be the heart and soul of the common man."

How do we again create an appreciation for the wit and wisdom, the intelligence and the talent of America's diverse peoples at the threshold of a new century? We face breathtaking change and challenges to our air, our water, our common places, and our heritage, to our democracy itself. To deal with these adequately we will need to renew the partnership between the people and our government.

Today, people often think of government as them, not us. People think of politics as something nasty and unpleasant — like a bad spectator sport. Americans need to remember that government is us, not them. We the people created it. It is our servant. Politics in its original meaning means "of the citizen." It is not simply elections. It is as good as we make it. It is about building our democratic way of life.

As Grant Stevensen suggested, all of us are called to participate in the development of the creative powers of the people. It is not a duty. It is rather a gift, an opportunity to be involved in the great public work of the early twenty-first century, building our collective powers to shape our future.

Tenth Civic Skill: Building Partnerships

Today, people tend to look at leaders either as saviors — or as enemies and idiots. This view reflects a perspective of either dependency or rebellion. Effective citizen efforts develop a partnership approach, like relationships among adults. What are called broad-based citizen organizations, like the ISAIAH group, refer to establishing public relationships with establishment leaders, whom many once saw simply as the enemy. They also refer to moving "from protest to governance," as described by Gerald Taylor, southern director of the Industrial Areas Foundation, an organizing network like ISAIAH's Gamaliel Foundation. "Moving into power means learning how to be accountable," said Taylor. "It means being able to negotiate and compromise. It means understanding that people are not necessarily evil because they have different interests or ways of looking at the world."

He tells the story of a group from the church-based citizen organization Baltimoreans United in Leadership Development (BUILD) when they first met with the senior senator from Maryland, Paul Sarbanes. Sarbanes pulled out his yellow pad and said, "I know about BUILD and your good work. What can I do for you?" They replied, "Nothing. We are here to get to know you. Why did you go into politics? What are your interests? We figure if we can learn about each other we will have a much more productive public relationship over time."[19]

TIPS AND TOOLS

Bringing leaders down to earth: Do a one-on-one with a leader in government, business, or some other major institution who might be intimidating to you. Ask why they went into their work. What have they learned? What are their tips for you, as a citizen actor and problem solver?

Stories: Is there a story in your community about citizens looking to government officials as saviors? Is there a story about people looking at government officials as enemies?

Your team: Hold a meeting on what it would take for your group to work with leaders as partners — neither saviors nor enemies. Figure out your own interests, values, and ideas before trying to go to the decision-making table.

Afterword
Culture and Power

Patterns of culture and power are germinating at the heart of the citizen movement. The movement shows how rich, rooted cultures can also be highly dynamic and full of change. As people gain power and civic capacity, they develop a sense of themselves as makers of culture, not simply inheritors of culture. This kind of power pattern is creative and expansive; it is "power to," not simply "power over."

THE CITIZEN MOVEMENT IN MINNESOTA SPANS THE conventional left-right spectrum. The widely different ideological perspectives represented by Wellstone Action and Republicans like former governor Al Quie and state senator Dave Senjem suggest the depth of the civic and populist tradition in Minnesota, and highlight the need for a theory of cultural change and power that goes beyond the conventional left-right spectrum.

Movements grounded in "the plain people" that develop the capacities of citizens to shape their destinies—to be agents and architects of their lives—are culturally based more than structurally based. Their agent is "the people," a different category than class or interest group. Such movements often grow from the sense that elites and impersonal forces are endangering the values, identities, and practices of a culturally constituted group of people, its memories, origins, common territory, and ways of life.

A sense of people-hood—including the sense of being Minnesotan—is understood through language, stories, symbols, oral traditions, foods, music, ways of remembering, and physical objects. A people may have a moment of birth, sacred texts, and important spaces. A people can also have multiple identities.

The cultural themes of civic politics based on "the people" will always be contested. We have seen many examples of defensive and reactive mobilizations in recent years using a populist rhetoric of "the people" against outside threats. But in democratic civic action, as people defend their ways of life they also develop as civic agents. If attended to, such cultural discontents provide immense resources for civic change and democratic renewal in an era like ours. A democratic perspective that focuses on what builds civic agency helps to make sense of the culture wars. It shows the need for a populist alternative to the defensive politics of grievance on the right and the thin economistic politics on the left—and the possibilities for a democratic renaissance.

Culture Theory on the Right: Buffers against Modernity

Conservative politics is associated with the theory that culture, which conservatives understand to be the ways of life that teach responsibility, loyalty, connection, initiative, and self-reliance, is under siege in the modern world. Such views grow from a long tradition of conservative thought, descending from writers like Alexis de Tocqueville and Edmund Burke, the English conservative who championed "little platoons" of communal life against the modern age. Conservatives have seen community-rooted settings as the bulwark of liberty and tradition against the winds of modernity.

Robert Nisbet, a pivotal figure for cultural conservatives, argued that Nazi Germany was the culminating fusion of state power and modernist culture, destroying all autonomous local structures: "All autonomous organizations were destroyed and made illegal: professions, service clubs, voluntary mutual aid groups, fraternal associations, even philatelist and musical societies. Such groups were regarded, and correctly, by the totalitarian government as potential sources of future resistance."[1]

Nisbet was a critic of big government, but he also emphasized the dangers of the capitalist marketplace. In his view, the market celebrates an acquisitive individualism that erodes the authority of the church, the family, and the neighborhood. It corrupts civic character, public honor, accountability, and respect for others. Capitalism alone produces a "sand heap of disconnected particles of humanity."[2]

By the beginning of the 1980s, conservatives such as Peter Berger and Richard Neuhaus, codirectors of the Mediating Structures Project of the American Enterprise Institute, were giving practical application to the idea of the colonizing, destructive power of government. To Berger and Neuhaus, big government "aspires to an all-comprehending jurisdiction." Acting out of its bureaucratic imperatives, justified by ideologies of equality, justice, and the public good, the state tends inevitably to expand its power, scope, and authority at the expense of such small-scale structures of daily life as families, churches, neighborhoods, and cultural and voluntary groups.

Stripped of any attachment to a particular background—religion, race, or group identity—the state is the ideal expression of professional culture and the "general will." But there is a terrible cost: "a growing trend toward legally enforced symbolic sterility in public space" that denies the authority of communities to make public their traditions and values, the weakening of family and small-group bonds, and the widening intrusions of experts and professionals into the most private realms of life. Accompanying such processes is the erosion of those buffers that protect the individual against the "mega-structures" of modern society.[3]

In Berger and Neuhaus's perspective, mediating structures are defensive buffers against the modern world. Intellectuals with a conservative cultural bent, such as Michael Joyce, William Schambra, Mary Ann Glendon, David Brooks, and Bob Woodson, have developed these themes in important ways. They see mediating structures of family, religious congregation, cultural and ethnic group, and neighborhood as threatened by social engineering and by liberalism that defines freedom as escape from communal restraint.

It is impossible to understand the "culture wars" without taking into account such cultural arguments, the anxieties and discontents they address, however defensively, and the lack of response by most progressives. Republicans made hay out of Democratic obliviousness to cultural discontents for a generation by speaking in populist accents — the reason for the journalistic equation of populism with Republicans like Ronald Reagan and George W. Bush. Thus, in the 1980 election, Reagan declared, "Thousands of towns and neighborhoods have seen their peace disturbed by bureaucrats and social planners through busing, questionable educational programs, and attacks on family." In his words, it was a time for "an end to giantism" and "a return of power to the people."[4]

Political and intellectual leaders on the right in the United States, Europe, and elsewhere have put progressives on the defensive with this kind of language. To understand why requires a look at cultural theory on the left.

Culture on the Left: Brake on Cosmopolitan Consciousness

In recent decades in the United States, left-oriented citizen action has often invoked populism. But its approach has also been highly economistic, that is, emphasizing the importance of economic matters with little sense of the relevance of cultural questions. Put differently, in recent years left-oriented "populist" criticisms of big business have often had little connection to cultural wellsprings of American democracy or discontents about the disruption of communal ties. As Dana Fisher shows in her recent book, *Activism, Inc.*, a technocratic disconnection from community has been common in techniques like the door-to-door canvassing by many issue-based citizen groups on the left, in which young staff appeal to people on the basis of issues but know little about community histories, networks, or cultures.

Recent left-oriented politics reflect an antitraditionalist cultural theory descended from the Enlightenment that took new form in the culturally uprooted activism of the late 1960s. From Enlightenment theorists of the eighteenth century onward, the tendency on the left has been to see the sundering of people's personal, communal, and historical identities—their "roots," in the words of the French philosopher Simone Weil—as a necessary, if tragic, prerequisite of cosmopolitan consciousness. Left intellectuals proposed, in place of community weakened or lost, community based on "new relationships."[5] While they were eloquent about human dislocations, both Karl Marx and Friedrich Engels saw the workers' break with rooted, communal traditions as necessary for progress. Marx called for a "radical rupture" from particular identities such as religion, place, and ethnicity. For Engels, "Tradition is the great retarding force . . . but being merely passive is sure to be broken down."[6]

Gianna Pomata has described differences between populist and socialist intellectual currents in Europe that were also found in the United States. "The Populists called into question one of the most basic tenets of European political thought—the belief in progress. . . . Populism and Marxism thus came to represent two contrasting positions." This difference included differing conceptions of the future and also of agency. The peasant class that Marx argued "represents barbarism inside civilization" was for Populists "the leadership in the struggle for a better future."[7]

If such views simply reflected notions of old-fashioned theorists they would make little difference now. But they have continued to shape the progressive imagination. On the socialist left, the view of cosmopolitan consciousness as a process of breaking with local, particular, national, and traditional identities has been the pattern, with exceptions like William Morris or Martin Buber here and there. The socialist view was succinctly summarized by Stanley Aronowitz in his essay entitled, appropriately enough, "The Working Class: A Break with the Past." According to Aronowitz, all particular identities of "race and nationality and sex and skill and industry" are obstacles to the development of cosmopolitan and oppositional consciousness.[8]

Such sentiments, in milder form, also infused liberal thought. The cultural stance of dominant strands of liberalism has held that enlightenment comes from intellectuals at the center, not the backwaters. Garry Wills expressed such a view in his critique of proposals for decentralized power. "The smaller the locale, the stricter the code; and this code . . . has always been at odds with the social openness, the chances for initiative, praised by liberals." In his reading, "What our history actually reveals at the community level is local conformity, rigid mores, religious and other prejudice, aristocracy and control."[9]

In the 1960s, such views became intertwined with generational experience to produce the distinctive stance of outsider to American cultural traditions. Youthful movements, with their sweeping alienation from mainstream America, its groups, symbols, stories, and traditions, found expression in the slogan, "Don't trust anyone over thirty," in the effort to create a counterculture, and in the sophisticated but disastrous 1968 generational statement by Paul Cowan, *The Making of an UnAmerican*. After the 1960s, a new generation of young activists worked to get beyond the hyperbole and open disdain for Americans that characterized the late 1960s. But the issue-focused approaches that came to characterize most progressive activism had little cultural rootedness.[10]

A dynamic lens on culture and power uncovers many democratic stirrings and signs of civic agency, as we have seen in *The Citizen Solution*. The question is how can these and other stirrings feed a larger movement. It is important to make the democratic theory of culture and power germinating in the new civic movement more explicit.

Toward a Civic Agency Theory of Culture and Power

Alternative practical, intellectual, and scholarly voices in recent years offer material for moving beyond static views of culture and for developing a theory of culture and power based on appreciation of the immense resources within individuals, communities, and societies.

A new generation of social historians concerned with the actual development of people's agency—how it is that ordinary people, steeped in experiences of subordination, develop the courage, spirit, skills, and confidence to assert themselves—has produced a history of the roots of movements with a great deal of nuance. Social history traditionally draws attention to the contradictory quality of community settings and cultural traditions, full of oppositional currents, democratic elements, and insurgent themes, as well as hierarchical and repressive ones. Some social historians are beginning to describe the ways in which powerless groups draw inspiration from cultural elements that many write off as simply oppressive.

Sara Evans and I, drawing on such social history as well as our experiences as Southerners in the civil rights movement (white Southerners in the movement, in my experience, had to come to terms with the ironies of culture in a way that many Northerners could avoid),[11] conceptualized the democratic potentials of culture with the idea of free spaces. The concept aims to show how powerless groups draw on and transform inherited resources as they develop public skills, public identities, and power.

We defined free spaces as places in the life of communities with public qualities, in which powerless groups have the capacity for self-organization, for engagement with alternative ideas, for developing public skills and identities. These actions entail new self-confidence, self-respect, and concern for the commonwealth. In free spaces, people create culture. They draw confidence from inherited traditions and also rework inherited symbols, ideas, and values to challenge ruling ideas. They turn aggrieved anger into positive agency.[12]

Thus, for instance, historian E. P. Thompson, in his work *The Making of the English Working Class*, described places such as taverns and sectarian churches in which working people found space for intellectual life and democratic self-organizations, separate from the gentry and the crown.[13] Women in nineteenth-century conservative but publicly active women's organizations defined in formal terms by domestic roles nonetheless found the free space to develop confidence and power. Confounding ideological categories, such groups laid the groundwork for twentieth-century suffrage.

In the long history of the African American freedom movement, blacks forged spaces for making a culture even in overwhelmingly oppressive settings, such as the slave system. Christianity was taught to slaves by slave owners in an effort to break their ties with African roots and socialize them into passive, docile roles. Yet Christianity provided rich materials, including work songs and gospel music, to use in fashioning strategies and language for everyday resistance. It also generated far-ranging radical insurgent visions of a transformed racial and political order based on stories like the Exodus narrative. Ideals of freedom and equality from the Declaration of Independence were also appropriated by a long line of black leaders.

A dynamic theory of culture is now appearing in anthropological and development literature. Vijayendra Rao and Michael Walton, editors of *Culture and Public Action*, an excellent recent book about United Nations and World Bank experiences in development work, challenge individualist, economistic, and technocratic frameworks that have dominated writings about development. Rao and Walton define culture as "about relationality—the relationships among individuals within groups, among groups, and between ideas and perspectives." This definition draws attention to locally rooted cultures and to their foundations in families, cultural groups, congregations, and the like, and also to larger cultural patterns in societies developing over long periods of time.[14]

They build on James Scott's *Seeing Like a State: How Certain Schemes to Improve the Human Condition Have Failed*. Scott, a scholar of peasant movements, shows how technocracy, or what he calls "high modernism," infused with egalitarian ideals and combined with state power and weak civil society, has devastated local cultures, mores, and relationships all over the world. The irony, in his view, is that this process has mainly been carried out by progressives with the best of liberal, egalitarian intentions.[15]

In *Culture and Public Action*, the authors argue that development workers, to be successful, must shift from one-size-fits-all technocratic interventions and instead recognize and tap the ingenuity and cultural resources of ordinary people in communities. In summation, they argue that this represents a shift from "equality of opportunity" to "equality of agency," in which development workers cease doing things *for* people and rather respect people's own capacities, helping to create "an enabling environment to provide the poor with the tools, and the voice, to navigate their way out of poverty.[16]

Amartya Sen and Arjun Appadurai in particular also stress the dynamic, future-oriented qualities of cultural systems at multiple levels from the local to the society-wide. Appadurai argues, "It is in culture that ideas of the future, as much as of those about the past, are embedded and nurtured."[17]

Combining insights drawn from recent cultural theory with participatory action research conducted with an affiliate of Shack Dwellers International, a poor people's housing organization, in Mumbai, India, Appadurai develops the concept of the "capacity to aspire" on the part of the poor. He proposes that, "in strengthening the capacity to aspire, conceived as a cultural capacity especially among the poor . . . the poor could find the resources required to contest and alter the conditions of their own poverty."

Appadurai stresses culture's open, interactive, fluid, dynamic, and created qualities. People's capacity to aspire is tied to "voice," the development of power and recognition that people gain through sustained organizing. "Voice must be expressed in terms of actions and performances which have local cultural force." The development of voice also means learning how to negotiate larger contexts. Such a process, in turn, can "change the terms of [people's] recognition, indeed the cultural framework itself."

To organize for voice and recognition requires cultural action and savvy strategic maneuvering. "There is no shortcut to empowerment. It has to take some local cultural form to have resonance, mobilize adherents, and capture the public space of debate." Organizing requires "efforts to change the dynamics . . . in their larger social worlds." A dynamic theory of culture suggests a capacity-oriented theory of power.

Power as Relational and Generative

In the free spaces of movements that develop civic agency, people have an experience of power that also confounds conventional views. Most power theories are based on models of power as one-way; the term "power" is largely synonymous with force, control, and rule. Power theory is based on scarce resource systems like land or money or the hypercompetitive scramble for prestige and position in universities. Such a view is present, for instance, in Steven Lukes's classic work, *Power: A Radical View.* Lukes takes what he calls a "three-dimensional view of power" and discusses not only power to get others to act and to prevent action but also power to make certain issues relevant and suppress others.[18]

Power is one-directional in such theories. Even power theories that are more relational usually conceive power as something imposed on people. Thus more recent theory in postmodern and critical studies has described the ways in which dominating power relationships are "encoded" in languages, practices, and identities. Michel Foucault is especially influential in this school of thought. Such power theory is rich with insight, but it pays little attention to the deepening of people's democratic agency, their capacity to act to shape their worlds.[19]

Academic theories rarely see power as what people do in relational, reciprocal interactions to get things done. Furthermore, there is no conception of the potential democratic power embedded in community life or in the motifs, stories, symbols, and narratives of the larger society. Critical theorists neglect power as a cultural resource that can be drawn upon and developed to challenge and transform dominant powers and relationships.

It would be naïve to ignore either the often extreme concentrations of power or the sometimes brutalizing operation of power in the modern world. Here, the most effective local organizing of recent years offers considerable insights. Leaders in broad-based organizing, such as Ed Chambers, Gerald Taylor, Sister Christine Stephens, Reverend Johnnie Ray Youngblood, Rom Coles, and others have sought to develop relational theories of power and politics. Organizers go back to the root of the word "power," from *poder,* meaning "to be able." They point out the sharp limits of academic theories of power because of their lack of attention to relationships.

Such organizers, leaders, and intellectuals argue that if one thinks about power as the capacity to act, not as something done to someone, power can be conceived of as relational, as two-way, even in situations of considerable inequality. For poor and working-class people, organizing for power means changing power dynamics to be more interactive and relational with leaders in politics and business, full of tension but also often productive results. Organizing involves developing the public capacities of relational leaders, most often women, at the center of community life.[20]

A dynamic theory of power creates a larger context than broad-based organizing because its goal is changing society, not simply building people's organizations that can win real gains. Populist theory must analyze cultural dynamics in the larger society, as well as the interpersonal and local dynamics of particular organizations. Cultural power, like information power, highlights power's generative, open qualities. Such power cannot be conceived adequately as a zero-sum force, power over. Cultural power is power to create—identities, narratives, practices. It can involve innovation or restoration. At the Center for Democracy and Citizenship, we have expressed the generative dimensions of power through the concept of citizenship as public work, highlighting the productive, not simply zero-sum qualities of politics that emphasize the fight over scarce resources.[21]

A view of the open-ended qualities of power also explains the potential catalytic power dynamics in government and in knowledge-based professions described in Chapters 9 and 10, where power is also a nonfinite relationship. In systems based on cultural and information-constituted authority, power can be dramatically increased as knowledge is pooled and cultural identities and relationships are brought into a public mix.

The New Civic Movement

Under the surface of trends that create widespread discouragement and feelings of powerlessness, there are signs of a new movement that is centrally about people's capacities to be agents and architects of their own lives. Thelma Craig, a remarkable civil rights leader in southern Alabama whose organization, the Civic League, elected more blacks to local office than anywhere else in the South, had insights of direct relevance to how we might see this movement develop. She believed that citizens must claim a sense of responsibility as well as power—in the words of the song popular in the civil rights era, "We Are the Ones We've Been Waiting For." Craig, a battler in the hard knocks school of Southern racial oppression, was one of the group of civil rights leaders who saw the need to build broad majorities by drawing out the democratic possibilities that exist within diverse communities.

Several years ago I heard Craig at a gathering in Nashville, Tennessee, of southern leaders working in broad-based citizen groups that resemble ISAIAH in Minnesota. "You have to begin with people who are dissatisfied with their position in life, find people who are willing to commit themselves, and are willing to confront the obstacles," she said. Craig had grown up and lived most of her life in the segregated South, with sharp limits on what African Americans could do or be, but in the 1960s she organized the Civic League of Alabama and had seen close up the impact of powerful organizing and civic action. "If you get a strong group, you can get recognition."[22]

"We had quite a few successes, and also some failures," Craig said. "Don't get discouraged by the failures. You can learn from them." She argued that real culture change requires a much broader view than simply looking at issues. "Good organizing like this has to have the good will of the community, the support of most everybody. Everybody will come together when there is a fire." She argued that there will always be opponents, hold-outs, and die-hards, but real change takes place when the overwhelming majority, perhaps four-fifths of the population, begins to see culture change as in their own interests.

Craig levied a prophetic critique that conveyed the idea of the citizen as co-creator of democracy. "What we didn't do is instill in young people enough the understanding that with power, you have to have responsibility." Reflecting on the tasks facing us today, she concluded, "We have moved from being a producer people to being consumers. We will need more organizing to move us back."

It is apparent to me that a powerful new citizen movement is stirring and growing in Minnesota and beyond. By taking part, we can learn to navigate our complicated lives, solve the challenging problems we face, and create healthy communities and a vibrant democratic society.

Notes

Introduction: Beyond Slash-and-Burn Politics (pages 3–9)

1. Jonathan Sacks, *The Politics of Hope* (London: Vintage, 2000), 47, xix.

2. Used originally in his speech to the nation outlining our future course on Nov. 9, 2001, this became a stock formulation. Thus, for instance, in his foreword to the *Life* magazine special issue, "The American Spirit: Meeting the Challenge of September 11," President Bush posed the rhetorical question, "What can I do to help in our fight?" and declared, "The answer is simple. All of us can become a September 11 volunteer."

3. David Frum, "Building a Coalition, Forgetting to Rule," *New York Times*, Aug. 14, 2007.

4. Adam Nagourney, "Legacy Laden with Protégés," *New York Times*, Aug. 14, 2007.

5. Franklin quoted in Richard Stengel, "A Time to Serve," *Time* magazine cover story, Sept. 10, 2007, p. 51.

6. Kelly Heskett, "Myself as a Citizen," quoted by Victor Bloomfield, Public Engagement Blog, May 19, 2007, http://blog.lib.umn.edu/victor/publicengagement.

Chapter 1: Working Together (pages 11–34)

1. Manning Marable, "Black History and the Vision of Democracy," in *The New Populism: The Politics of Empowerment*, ed. Harry C. Boyte and Frank Riessman (Philadelphia: Temple University Press, 1986), 202–3.

2. Marie Ström, Institute for Democracy in South Africa, 2006, in collaboration with the CDC, handout in author's possession.

3. This account is adapted from Harry C. Boyte and Nan Kari, "Unsung

Heroes," *New Democrat* (July-Aug. 1997): 13–17, and "Taking the Public Out of Public Art," *Wall Street Journal*, Aug. 6, 1997.

4. Richard C. Harwood, "The Nation's Looking Glass," *Kettering Review* (Spring 2000): 15–16, 7–8.

5. Dean Mohs, *Celebrating and Encouraging Community Involvement of Older Minnesotans: A Snapshot of Current Minnesota Baby Boomers and Older Adults.* Minnesota Board of Aging, report in author's possession, Apr. 2000, p. 3, 6.

6. Joan Didion, *Political Fictions* (New York: Knopf, 2001), 28, 279, 253–54.

7. Donna Shalala, David Dodds Henry Lecture at University of Illinois, 1989, transcript in author's possession.

8. Email correspondence, Dec. 11, 2007.

9. This observation about the parallels with Eastern Europeans under communism was made by David Mathews, president of the Kettering Foundation, in a conversation about positivism in 1999. See also Harry C. Boyte, "The Struggle against Positivism," *Academe* 86:4 (Aug. 2000), online at http://www.aaup.org/AAUP/pubsres/academe/2000/JA/Feat/Boyt.htm.

10. Hubert Humphrey, *Education of a Public Man: My Life and Politics* (Garden City: Doubleday, 1976).

11. Ibid., 8–10.

12. Quoted from Humphrey Institute student video. Presented to the Graduation Party at the Humphrey Institute, May 8, 2004, Minneapolis.

13. Thomas Bender, *Intellect and Public Life: Essays on the Social History of Academic Intellectuals in the United States* (Baltimore, MD: Johns Hopkins University Press, 1993).

14. Drawn from Harry Boyte, *Civic Engagement News* #11, electronic newsletter of the Council on Public Engagement, 2004; *Strong Families, Strong Schools* (U.S. Department of Education, 1994), details the survey findings of Nathan and Betty Radcliffe, showing that 21 percent of 1,823 elementary and secondary school educators rated their preparation for working with parents effective or very effective. Recent research by Nathan's Center for School Change (2007), interviewing minority groups, the Minnesota state PTA, and others, found 91 percent said recent teacher graduates are not very prepared or not at all prepared to involve parents and families.

15. Castells quoted in David Brooks, "The Next Culture War," *New York Times*, June 12, 2007.

16. Jim Gambone and Erica Whittlinger, *The Seventy-Five Percent Factor: Uncovering Hidden Boomer Values*, 2002 study, on the Web at www.refirement.com/pages/executivesummarypage.html; *Christian Science Monitor*, Dec. 23, 1977; Harry C. Boyte, *The Backyard Revolution: Understanding the New Citizen Movement* (Philadelphia: Temple University Press, 1980).

17. For a rich chronicling by a major architect and organizer of the movement Project for Public Spaces, see www.publicspaces.org.

18. These trends are documented on the Community Wealth website, www.community-wealth.org; see also Gar Alperovitz, "The Wealth of Neighborhoods," *Democracy: A Journal of Ideas* (Summer 2006): 19–32.

19. This history is taken from the Citizens League website, http://www.citizensleague.org, accessed July 18, 2007.

20. Telephone interview with Sean Kershaw, July 18, 2007.

21. From the Citizens League MAP 150 description, www.citizensleague.org, accessed July 18, 2007.

22. Adapted from *By the People, Citizenship Curriculum for AmeriCorps,* by the Center for Democracy and Citizenship, http://www.cpn.org/tools/manuals/Youth/americorps3.html; building on Melissa Bass, Harry Boyte, et al., *Making the Rules: A Public Achievement Guild Book,* (Minneapolis: Project Public Life/ Humphrey Institute, 1989); third edition on web at http://www.cpn.org/tools/manuals/Youth/rules1.html.

Chapter 2: Minnesota's Living Civic Culture (pages 35–45)

1. Nina Archabal, introduction to *Minnesota, Real and Imagined: Essays on the State and Its Culture,* ed. Stephen R. Graubard (St. Paul: Minnesota Historical Society Press, 2001), ix.

2. Ben Arnoldy, "Minneapolis Shows Why It's Rated No. 1 in Volunteerism," *Christian Science Monitor,* Aug. 8, 2007.

3. Archabal, Introduction, vix.

4. Kolderie, speech to the St. Paul Skylight Club, Jan. 18, 2006; quoted from p. 2, transcript in author's possession.

5. Paul Nussbaum, "Environment Is Uniting Left and Right," *Philadelphia Inquirer,* Mar. 22, 2005.

6. Interview with Timothy DenHerder-Thomas, St. Paul, June 5, 2007.

7. Interview with Lt. Col. Timothy Kamenar, Minneapolis, June 7, 2007, and written correspondence, Sept. 28, 2007; elaborated with examples from the Warrior to Citizen section of the CDC website, www.publicwork.org, accessed July 28, 2007.

Chapter 3: Breaking the Silence (pages 47–59)

1. Walter Mondale, *The Changing Shape of Minnesota* (Minneapolis: Humphrey Institute, 2003).

2. These views are quoted from Harry C. Boyte, *Public Engagement in a*

Civic Mission (Washington, D.C.: Council on Public Policy Education, 1999); department chair quoted on page 6.

3. House meeting at University of Minnesota, Minneapolis campus, Sept. 19, 2005.

4. Willey, email correspondence, Oct. 25, 2005.

5. East African Circle, Nov. 14, 2005; comments from author's observation of Somali student forum, Nov. 10, 2005, University of Minnesota Leadership class.

6. Peg Chemberlin, prepared remarks, House meeting with state legislators, May 11, 2006, Minnesota State Capitol.

7. Here and below, Alina Tugend, "Pining for the Kick-Back Weekend," *New York Times,* Apr. 15, 2006, accessed online Apr. 18, 2006.

8. Doherty, on edginess, from personal conversations.

9. Interview with Andrea Grazzini Walstrom, Minneapolis, May 30, 2006.

10. Mary Lynn Smith, "Wanted: A Day of Rest for Youth Sports," *Minneapolis Star Tribune,* Oct. 2, 2005.

11. Here and below, Walstrom interview.

12. Grace, Mereness, and Dubbles quoted in Smith, "Wanted: A Day of Rest."

13. Walstrom interview.

14. Interview with Gail Dubrow, July 16, 2006.

Chapter 4: A History of Adventurous Experiment (pages 61–76)

1. *WPA Federal Writers Project Guide to Minnesota 1938* (St. Paul: Minnesota Historical Society Press, 1938, 1983), 7.

2. Rhoda Gilman, "The History and Peopling of Minnesota: Its Culture," in *Minnesota Real and Imagined,* ed. Stephen R. Graubard, 26.

3. Charles Rumford Walker, *American City: A Rank and File History of Minneapolis* (Minneapolis: University of Minnesota Press, 2005); editor quoted on p. 11.

4. Walker, *American City,* 29.

5. Ibid., 11.

6. Special 75th anniversary issue of *St. Paul Pioneer Press,* Dec. 31, 1933.

7. Here and paragraphs below, Jim Storm and Michael Vitt, *Master of Creative Philanthropy: The Story of Russell V. Ewald* (Minneapolis: Philanthroid Press, 2000), 10, 11, 58–59, 106.

8. John Dewey, *Collected Works,* vol. 6, p. 232. Thank you to Jim Farr for these references to Dewey's explicit views on populism.

9. Norman K. Risjord, *A Popular History of Minnesota* (St. Paul: Minnesota Historical Society Press, 2005), 213.

10. Nan Kari and I trace these cooperative work traditions in the experiences and cultures of immigrant groups in *Building America: The Democratic Promise of Public Work* (Philadelphia: Temple, 1996).

11. My student Stephanie Conduff, from the Cherokee Nation of Oklahoma and a close student of Indian history, argues compellingly that Native peoples had values and outlook with strong populist characteristics.

12. *WPA Guide*, 77–78; second immigrant quoted from William E. Lass, *Minnesota: A History*, 2nd ed. (New York: W.W. Norton, 1998), 143.

13. Thomas O'Connell, "Toward a Cooperative Commonwealth: An Introductory History of the Farmer-Labor Movement in Minnesota" (PhD diss., Union Graduate School, Cincinnati, 1979).

14. Ibid., 17,

15. Ibid., 138–44, 155–56.

16. John Radzilowski, *On-the-Road Histories: Minnesota* (Northampton, MA: Interlink Books, 2006), 48.

17. Quoted in Ibid., 49.

18. "Immigration Reform Campaign Heats Up," *ISAIAH: Building Just Communities* (Apr. 2006): 1, 4; David D. Kirkpatrick, "Demonstrations on Immigration Harden a Divide," *New York Times*, Apr. 17, 2006; interview with Jacqueline Belzer, June 15, 2006, Minneapolis.

19. Here and below, Stephanie Devitt, "Northeast Neighborhood House: Research report for the Center for Democracy and Citizenship," Dec. 10, 2006, in author's possession, p. 4, 6.

20. Lori Sturdevant, ed., *Changemaker: W. Harry Davis* (Afton, MN: Afton Historical Society Press, 2003), 32.

21. Kay Miller, Richard Green—The Minneapolis school superintendent believes 'When the public schools have failed and ceased or are weakened this nation will have failed,'" *Minneapolis Star Tribune*, Sept. 7, 1986.

Chapter 5: Cultural Leaders (pages 77–88)

1. For another example of this thinking, see Paul Tough's article in the *New York Times Magazine*, "What It Takes to Make a Student," Nov. 26, 2006. The trade-off between community and individual achievement is simply taken as a given of modern society.

2. Interview with Atum Azzahir, Minneapolis, May 23, 2006.

3. Quote from Minnesota Working Group discussion, Apr. 13, 2006.

4. Quotes from Cultural Wellness Center website, http://www.ppcwc .org/about_us, accessed Feb. 2, 2008.

5. See for instance, Walt Whitman, *Leaves of Grass*, edited by Harold W. Blodgett and Sculley Bradley (New York: New York University, 1965).

6. Quotes from interview with Atum Azzahir, May 23, 2006, Minneapolis. Material from Azzahir and Barbee taken from Atum Azzahir and Janice Barbee, "Powderhorn Phillips Cultural Wellness Center: Cultural Reconnection and Community Building for Personal and Community Health," in *The End of One Way* (Minneapolis: McKnight Foundation, 2004), 44–61.

7. Interview, May 23, 2006.

8. Azzahir and Barbee, "Powderhorn Phillips Cultural Wellness Center," 50.

9. Here and below, author's notes from meeting of Minnesota Works Together working group, Apr. 13, 2006.

10. Here and below, interview, May 23, 2006.

11. Ira De Reid, *The Negro Community of Baltimore: A Social Survey* (Baltimore: Urban League, 1934); interview with Gerald Taylor, Baltimore, Nov. 11, 1987; interview with Vernon Dobson, Baltimore, Nov. 13, 1987.

12. Azzahir quotes above from interview, May 23, 2006.

Chapter 6: ISAIAH's Worldview (pages 89 – 105)

1. "Immigration Reform Campaign Heats Up," *ISAIAH: Building Just Communities* (Apr. 2006): 1, 4; a booklet for the Faith in Democracy meeting in author's possession; David D. Kirkpatrick, "Demonstrations on Immigration Harden a Divide," *New York Times,* Apr. 17, 2006; interview with Jacqueline Belzer, June 15, 2006, Minneapolis.

2. For descriptions, see Harry C. Boyte, *Backyard Revolution: Understanding the New Citizen Movement* (Philadelphia: Temple, 1980); Boyte, *Community Is Possible: Repairing America's Roots* (New York: Harper & Row, 1984); Boyte, *Common Wealth: A Return to Citizen Politics* (New York: Free Press, 1990); and Boyte, *Everyday Politics: Reconnecting Citizens and Public Life* (Philadelphia: University of Pennsylvania Press, 2004).

3. Quoted from the Faith in Democracy booklet, in author's possession; also on the ISAIAH website, http://www.gamaliel.org/isaiah/whoweare/whatisisaiah.htm, accessed Feb. 2, 2008.

4. Personal conversation, St. Paul, May 11, 2006.

5. Interview with Doran Schrantz, Minneapolis, May 23, 2006.

6. Interview with Sarah Mullins, St. Paul, June 1, 2006.

7. *Faith in Democracy* (Minneapolis: ISAIAH, 2004), 16.

8. Ibid.

9. Here and below, Grant Stevensen, keynote address at the Faith in Democracy conference, Oct. 10, 2004, text in author's possession.

10. Interview with Aneesa Parks, Minneapolis, June 13, 2006.

11. *Faith in Democracy,* 16. Also on web at http://www.gamaliel.org/isaiah/whoweare/whatisisaiah.htm, accessed Feb. 3, 2008.

12. Saul Alinsky, *Reveille for Radicals* (New York: Random House, 1946), 76, 79.

13. Here and below, interview with Ron Peterson, Roseville, MN, June 13, 2006.

14. Interview with Doran Schrantz, Minneapolis, May 23, 2006.

15. Interview with Aneesa Parks, June 13, 2006.

16. Telephone interview with Nora Slawik, Maplewood, MN, June 22, 2006.

17. Quotes above taken from author's notes of conversation with Myron Orfield, Mar. 19, 2006, New Brighton, MN.

18. Personal conversation with Ayers, Mar. 21, 2006, Minneapolis; interview with Sara Gleason, St. Paul, June 1, 2006.

19. Interview with Sue Eng, Minneapolis, May 9, 2006; interview with Doran Schrantz, Minneapolis, June 21, 2006.

Chapter 7: Everyday Politics (pages 107–123)

1. Taylor Branch, *Pillar of Fire: America in the King Years, 1963–1965* (New York: Simon & Schuster, 1998), 77.

2. Information adapted from Harry C. Boyte presentation at the American Political Science Association, Sept. 2, 2001, San Francisco. http://www.publicwork.org/pdf/speeches/TaleofTw.pdf.

3. Michael Kuhne, "Public Achievement Teaching Circle: Introducing the Core Concepts of Public Achievement," a discussion guide for faculty at Minneapolis Community and Technical College (MCTC), Feb. 2003, 3.

4. Here and below, student quotes from Michael Kuhne, *Listening to the Students' Voices: An Early Document in the Ongoing Assessment of the Relationship between Public Achievement and the Urban Teacher Program* (Minneapolis: MCTC, 2001), 5, 6, 18.

5. June Knobbe's remarks in Leadership Minor/Public Achievement forum, Minneapolis, June 30, 2006.

6. Student Council on Public Engagement vision statement, accessed on

Victor Bloomfield's Public Engagement blog, Mar. 29, 2006, http://blog.lib.umn.edu/victor/publicengagement.

7. Interview with Russ Lyons, Minneapolis, Apr. 14, 2006.

8. Laila Davis, "Creating Sustainable Engagement from Public Forums," Humphrey Institute professional paper, July 25, 2006, p. 29.

9. Martha Bayles, "Now Showing: The Good, the Bad, and the Ugly," *Washington Post,* Aug. 28, 2005, B01.

10. Here and below, interview with Amy Jo Pierce, Minneapolis, June 1, 2006.

11. Here and below, interview with Blake Hogan, Minneapolis, Apr. 27, 2006.

12. Here and below, interview with Amir Pinnix, June 16, 2006.

Chapter 8: From Isolation to Neighborhood Communities (pages 125–142)

1. Jefferson and Rush quoted from People's Bicentennial Commission, *Voices of the American Revolution* (New York: Bantam Books, 1974), 175–76; Paul Leichester Ford, ed., *The Works of Thomas Jefferson* (New York: Knickerbocker Press, 1903), 278.

2. David Mathews, "Public-Government/Public-Schools," *National Civic Review* 85, no. 3 (Fall 1996): 15; Peter Levine, *The Future of Democracy: Developing the Next Generation of American Citizens* (Boston: Tufts University Press, 2007), 110.

3. David Mathews, *Reclaiming Public Education by Reclaiming Our Democracy* (Dayton, OH: Kettering Foundation Press, 2006), 16–18.

4. Annette Lareau, *Unequal Childhoods: Class, Race, and Family Life* (Berkeley: University of California Press, 2003), 4, 5, 24, 35.

5. Figures from Nick Longo, *Why Community Matters: Connecting Education with Civic Life* (Albany: State University of New York Press, 2007), 135.

6. Nan Skelton, Nan Kari, Kari Dennisen, David Scheie, and Harry Boyte, *A Community Alive with Learning* (Minneapolis: Humphrey Institute, 2006), 6; organizer quoted in Longo, *Why Community Matters,* 143.

7. *Community Alive with Learning,* 7.

8. Laurence Steinberg, *Beyond the Classroom: Why School Reform Has Failed and What Parents Need to Do* (New York: Simon & Schuster, 1996), 194.

9. Street-Stewart quoted in Longo, *Why Community Matters,* 101.

10. Dennis Shirley, *Community Organizing for Urban School Reform* (Austin: University of Texas Press, 1997), 72.

11. Longo, *Why Community Matters,* 102; Stein quote, p. 101.

12. Quoted from Boyte, "Libraries as Free Spaces," *Continuum* (May 2006), 1.

13. From unpublished Jane Addams School evaluation interviews by Michael Baizerman, University of Minnesota, 2000, in author's possession.

14. Ibid.

15. This account is enriched by Nick Longo's *Why Community Matters,* as well as author's direct observations; Benitez quote, p. 140.

16. Skelton quoted from Harry C. Boyte, *Everyday Politics: Reconnecting Citizens and Public Life* (Philadelphia: University of Pennsylvania Press, 2004), 152.

17. Quoted in *A Community Alive with Learning,* 19.

18. Ibid., 21.

19. Quoted in Longo, *Why Community Matters,* 92; Cudahy quote, 104.

20. Myron P. Medcalf, "A Better Education Just a Bus Ride Away," *Minneapolis Star Tribune,* July 3, 2007.

21. Adapted from "Citizenship in the Community," a guide by Harry Boyte and Robert Hildreth, developed by the Center for Democracy and Citizenship for the Boy Scouts, 2002.

Chapter 9: Citizen Professionals (pages 143–157)

1. Costello, *Professional Identity Crisis: Race, Class Gender, and Success at Professional School* (Nashville: Vanderbilt University Press, 2005).

2. Here and other references to Laurie McGinnis below, see Laurie McGinnis, "Transportation Professional as Citizen Professional: Creating Vital Places," independent study paper, June 2006, Humphrey Institute.

3. Excerpt from an interview with William Doherty, Minneapolis, July 22, 2001.

4. Interview with William Doherty, St. Paul, June 28, 2006.

5. Here and below, William J. Doherty, "Community Engaged Parent Education," Report to the McKnight Foundation, Dec. 7, 2004, in author's possession.

6. Interview with Eric Yancey, Minneapolis, June 2, 2006.

7. Here and below, interview with William Doherty, Jan. 24, 2007, Minneapolis; horror stories from Patrick Condon, "Simple Birthdays for Kids Are the Goal," *Minneapolis Star Tribune,* Jan. 22, 2007; Barnes' story from Editor's Corner, "Local Parent Group Hopes to Bring Sanity Back to Kids' Birthdays," *Minneapolis Star Tribune,* Jan. 23, 2007.

Chapter 10: Renewing Government of the People (pages 159–173)

1. "Minnesota Shows Signs of Civic Revival," *Star Tribune*, Oct. 29, 2005.

2. Interview with Elizabeth Kautz, Burnsvile, MN, Aug. 10, 1995.

3. Kautz quotes from interview, Aug. 10, 1995; Konat quotes from Harry C. Boyte and Nancy N. Kari, "Commonwealth Democracy," *Dissent* (Fall, 1997): 49.

4. Frank Benest, "Serving Customers or Engaging Citizens: What Is the Future of Local Government?" This article was originally published as part of a special insert in the International City/County Management Association Journal, Nov. 1996. It is on the web at http://www.vcn.bc.ca/citizens-handbook/benest.html, accessed Feb. 3, 2008.

5. Herbert Croly, *The Promise of American Life* (New York: Macmillan, 1909), 139, 453.

6. Jane Addams, *On Education* (New Brunswick: Transaction Publishers, reprinted 1994), 98.

7. Liberty Hyde Bailey, *New York State Rural Problems* (Albany: J.B. Lon, 1913), 11–12, 133.

8. Liberty Hyde Bailey, *The State and the Farmer* (New York: MacMillan, 1908), 1, 120.

9. Ibid., 173–74.

10. Material from Pat Borich's presentation at the first Reinventing Citizenship meeting, held at the White House, Jan. 14, 1994, author's notes.

11. Interview with Carol Shields, St. Paul, June 15, 1995.

12. Mobley quoted in Harry C. Boyte and Nancy N. Kari, *Building America: The Democratic Promise of Public Work* (Philadelphia: Temple University Press, 1996), 197.

13. Material on Extension adapted from Harry C. Boyte and Nancy N. Kari, "Democracy of the People: Expanding Citizen Capacity," in *Capacity for Change? The Nonprofit World in the Age of Devolution*, ed. Dwight F. Burlingame, William A. Diaz, and Warren F. Ilchman (Indianapolis: Center on Philanthropy, 1997); Salzer quote, 120.

14. For a detailed summary of findings and key lessons, see Carmen Sirianni and Lewis Friedland, *Civic Innovation in America: Community Empowerment, Public Policy, and the Movement for Civic Renewal* (Berkeley: University of California Press, 2001), and their website, www.cpn.org; for the Camp David meeting on the future of democracy, see my log at http://www.public work.org/pdf/travellogs/Camp%20David%20seminar_386.pdf, and Benjamin Barber's account of these experiences in *The Truth of Power: Intellectual Affairs in the Clinton White House* (New York: W.W. Norton, 2001).

15. Carmen Sirianni, *Investing in Democracy*, manuscript in progress, Chapter 4, pp. 7, 28, in author's possession.

16. Email from Senjem to author, Aug. 10, 2006.

17. Interview with Nora Slawik, June 22, 2006.

18. Email from Senjem to author, Aug. 10, 2006.

19. Interview with Gerald Taylor, Apr. 26, 2002, Durham, NC.

Afterword: Culture and Power (pages 175–187)

1. Robert Nisbet, "The Total Community," in *Power in Societies*, ed. Marvin Olson (New York: Macmillan, 1970), 423.

2. Ibid.

3. Peter Berger and Richard John Neuhaus, *To Empower People: The Role of Mediating Structures in Public Policy* (Washington, D.C: American Enterprise Institute, 1977), 6; Reagan quotes from George Will, "Grinchiness at Christmas Time," *Minneapolis Tribune*, Dec. 24, 1979.

4. Ronald Reagan, quoted in William Schambra, *The Quest for Community and the Quest for a New Public Philosophy* (Washington, D.C.: American Enterprise Institute, 1983), 30.

5. Weil and some others who observed and challenged this pattern of left deracination are described in *Common Wealth: A Return to Citizen Politics*, ed. Harry C. Boyte (New York: Free Press, 1980); *Everyday Politics: Reconnecting Citizens and Public Life* (Philadelphia: University of Pennsylvania Press, 2004); and, with Nan Kari, in *Building America: The Democratic Promise of Public Work* (Philadelphia: Temple University Press, 1996).

6. Karl Marx, *The Holy Family* (Moscow: Foreign Language Publishers, 1956), 123; Friedrich Engels, *The Housing Question* (Moscow: Progress, 1970), 29.

7. Gianna Pomata, "A Common Heritage," in Harry C. Boyte and Frank Riessman, eds., *The New Populism: The Politics of Empowerment* (Philadelphia: Temple University Press, 1986), 35–36.

8. Stanley Aronowitz, "The Working Class: A Break with the Past," in *Divided Society: The Ethnic Experience in America*, ed. Colin Greer (New York: Basic Books, 1974), 312–13.

9. Garry Wills, *Nixon Agonistes: The Crisis of the Self-Made Man* (New York: New American Library, 1969), 463, 468.

10. I describe this dynamic in *Everyday Politics*, building in part on an unpublished article on the new populism written for *The Nation* with Nan Kari.

11. Robert Coles, a Harvard psychologist, gives a fascinating account of his

own realization of this dynamic as he worked in a Freedom House in Mississippi in 1964 in "A Working People's Politics," in Boyte and Reissman, *The New Populism*, 83–99.

12. Sara M. Evans and Harry C. Boyte, *Free Spaces: The Sources of Democratic Change in America* (New York: Harper & Row, 1986; Chicago: Chicago University Press, 1992).

13. E. P. Thompson, *The Making of the English Working Class* (New York: Vintage, 1966).

14. Vijayendra Rao and Michael Walton, "Culture and Public Action," in *Culture and Public Action*, ed. Rao and Walton (Stanford: Stanford University Press, 2004), 5.

15. James C. Scott, *Seeing Like a State: How Certain Schemes to Improve the Human Condition Have Failed* (New Haven, CN: Yale University Press, 1998).

16. Rao and Walton, "Conclusion," in *Culture and Public Action*, 361.

17. Here and below, Arjun Appadurai, "The Capacity to Aspire," in *Culture and Public Action*, 60–62, 69.

18. Steven Lukes, *Power: A Radical View* (New York: Macmillan, 1974).

19. See for instance, Andrew Ross, *Universal Abandon: The Politics of Postmodernism* (Minneapolis: University of Minnesota Press, 1988); Linda Alcoff, "Cultural Feminism Versus Post-Structuralism: The Identity Crisis in Feminist Theory," *Signs: Journal of Women in Culture and Society* 13 (1988): 405–36; on Foucault, see for instance, *Discipline and Punish: The Birth of the Prison* (New York: Vintage, 1975).

20. This argument about relational power was developed in Bernard Loomer, "Two Conceptions of Power," *Criterion* 15 (1976): 12–29, a piece widely used in organizing, especially by the Industrial Areas Foundation.

21. See for instance, Harry C. Boyte, "Civic Populism," *Perspectives on Politics* 1 (2003): 737–42.

22. Here and below, Craig's presentation to the southern regional leadership meeting of the Industrial Areas Foundation, Nashville, TN, Nov. 12, 1999.

Index

The Citizen Solution was designed and set in Fournier type
by Christopher Kuntze, Whitefield, New Hampshire.
Printed by Friesens, Altona, Manitoba.